Green Technologies

Scan to see all titles in the series.

East Asia and Pacific Development Studies

Green Technologies

Decarbonizing Development in
East Asia and Pacific

Francesca de Nicola
Aaditya Mattoo
Trang Thu Tran

WORLD BANK GROUP

ISBN (paper): 978-1-4648-2198-1
ISBN (electronic): 978-1-4648-2217-9
DOI: 10.1596/978-1-4648-2198-1

Cover image: © Ravi Salim. Artwork by Ahmad Sadali, "Lelehan Emas Pada Relief Gunungan" (Drips of Gold Upon the Relief of a Mountain), 1973, mixed media on canvas. Collection of Museum of Modern and Contemporary Art in Nusantara (Museum MACAN). Image courtesy of Museum MACAN. Used with permission. Further permission required for reuse.

About the artist: Ahmad Sadali (1924–1987) was a central figure in the development of modern art in Indonesia. He used painting as a means to express his instinctive connection with nature (https://artagendasea.org/artists /35-ahmad-sadali/overview/).

Cover design: Guillaume Musel, Pi COMM, France / Bill Pragluski, Critical Stages, LLC

Library of Congress Control Number: 2025935437

EAST ASIA AND PACIFIC DEVELOPMENT STUDIES

The EAST ASIA AND PACIFIC DEVELOPMENT STUDIES explore economic issues in one of the most vibrant regions at a time of rapid technological change. Topics range from improving productivity and jobs to advancing services reform, and from enhancing education and health care to facilitating the green transition. Each volume blends analysis, examples, and policy lessons of interest to scholars, policy makers, and practitioners.

TITLES IN THE SERIES

Firm Foundations of Growth: Productivity and Technology in East Asia and Pacific (2025)

Future Jobs: Robots, Artificial Intelligence, and Digital Platforms in East Asia and Pacific (2025)

Green Technologies: Decarbonizing Development in East Asia and Pacific (2025)

Services Unbound: Digital Technologies and Policy Reform in East Asia and Pacific (2024)

Fixing the Foundation: Teachers and Basic Education in East Asia and Pacific (2023) (World Bank East Asia and Pacific Regional Report)

All books in this series are available for free in the World Bank's Open Knowledge Repository at https://hdl.handle.net/10986/42047.

Contents

Maps

Tables

Foreword

What East Asia and Pacific (EAP) does to reduce emissions will shape the world's transition to a lower carbon economy. The region is already the engine behind many of the world's green technologies, driving innovation and scaling up manufacturing in solar panels, batteries, and electric vehicles (EVs). But its own emissions make up 40 percent of global emissions and continue to rise, even as the domestic adoption of green technologies lags its global export success.

Renewables and EVs have seen impressive growth in some countries: solar photovoltaic capacity in Viet Nam jumped from nearly zero to almost 25 percent between 2018 and 2020, while China's share of EVs in the vehicle stock more than doubled from 2020 to 2022—but the region remains heavily reliant on fossil fuels. Many developing EAP countries continue to subsidize fossil fuels and hesitate to penalize carbon-intensive technologies, like much of the rest of the world.

In a series of new books, the EAP region of the World Bank is examining how technological advances are impacting firm growth, productivity, jobs, services, and the transition to low-carbon economies. This book explores how EAP can build on its strength in green innovation and manufacturing to accelerate decarbonization.

Policy choices today are important because technological progress is not exogenous; early innovation and adoption help drive down future costs. On average, the cost of solar, wind, and batteries dropped exponentially, at a rate of almost 10 percent a year since they were first marketed, and deployment increased at about the same pace. In contrast, fossil fuel technologies, such as coal, oil, and gas, have seen no significant decline in cost since 1880. Getting incentives right can shift the trajectory of both emissions and technology adoption toward a better balance between the short-term costs of the transition and long-term economic growth.

The book offers practical policy options going forward. For technologies that are already economically viable, removing policy distortions such as fossil fuel subsidies and import tariffs on green goods offers win-wins that countries can prioritize. Similar benefits can be reaped by addressing market failures, such as inadequate information in credit markets about the viability of green technologies or the difficulty private firms face in coordinating investments in shared green infrastructure.

Where technologies are not yet viable, advances can, in principle, be made by providing incentives to encourage the adoption of green technologies—for example, through carbon pricing that addresses the environmental externalities. But these interventions deliver environmental improvements at an economic cost. How far EAP countries are willing to go will depend on the commitments they have already made, the returns they receive (such as domestic gains from learning-by-doing and health co-benefits), and actions by the rest of the world (in terms of commitments to reduce emissions and provide financial and technical assistance). In all cases, the book underscores the need for complementary measures to ensure the transition is inclusive: examples include supporting low-income households to cope with higher prices and helping workers in fossil fuel sectors retrain for new opportunities.

I hope readers of this book will come away with reasons for optimism about the progress and potential of green technology in the region. The cost of many of the green technologies we need has come down faster than expected: between 2010 and 2022, the cost of solar power fell by 89 percent, and that of offshore wind power fell by 59 percent. But we must move faster to deploy them and support newer technologies to come to the market. Through this analysis, I hope policy makers, researchers, and practitioners will find insights and inspiration to implement the deeper domestic reforms needed to facilitate the green transition and to engage in international cooperation on climate, innovation, and trade in green goods.

Manuela V. Ferro
Vice President, East Asia and Pacific
The World Bank

Acknowledgments

This book is a product of the Office of the Chief Economist, East Asia and Pacific Region of the World Bank.

Analyses in selected chapters are based on research conducted by the authors jointly with Yu Cao, Unnada Chewpreecha, and Hector Pollitt. Alicia Huong Dang, Kala Krishna, Meng Yu Ngov, Pierre-Louis Vézina, and Yingyan Zhao contributed to background research. Sarah Waltraut Hebous and Felipe Yudi Yamashita Roviello provided excellent research assistance. We also thank Yiyi Bai, Duong Trung Le, and Miles McKenna for their contribution to selected data and analyses used in the book.

Manuela Ferro provided valuable guidance and helpful comments. We are grateful for the helpful comments from the peer reviewers: Richard Damania, Stephane Hallegatte, Ralf Martin, and Penelope Ann Mealy. The manuscript also benefited from comments by Cristian Aedo, Omar Arias, Marcio Cruz, Ergys Islamaj, Denis Medvedev, Martino Pelli, and Katherine Stapleton as well as from members of the World Bank's East Asia and Pacific Management Team.

We thank Maria Laura Gonzalez Canosa for leading the communications strategy, Narya Ou and Cecile Wodon for their administrative support. Barbara Karni copy edited the manuscript, and Gwenda Larsen proofread the book. Caroline Polk was the production editor. Cindy Fisher and Patricia Katayama provided advice and guidance on the publication process. Geetanjali S. Chopra, Ngan Hong Nguyen, Yi Gu and other members of the External Communications team helped with dissemination.

The cover features "Lelehan Emas Pada Relief Gunungan" (Drips of Gold Upon the Relief of a Mountain), by Ahmad Sadali, a mixed-media composition in the collection of the Museum of Modern and Contemporary Art in Nusantara (MACAN), Indonesia. We would like to thank Sade Bimantara, Carolyn Sinulingga, and Svetlana A. Prasasthi, as well as the team at the Embassy of Indonesia, for facilitating the connection with Museum MACAN and for their kind support throughout the process. We are also grateful to Venus Lau, Amalia Wirjono, Chabib Hapsoro, and the Museum MACAN team for providing the high-quality image for the cover and connecting us with Ravi Salim, to whom we are deeply grateful for permission to feature Ahmad Sadali's artwork.

About the authors

Francesca de Nicola is a senior economist in the Economic and Market Research Unit of the International Finance Corporation. Her current research focuses on productivity, innovation, and the green transition. She started her career at the International Food Policy Research Institute. She has published in journals such as the *Journal of Development Economics, Quantitative Economics,* and *Energy Economics*. She holds a PhD in economics from Johns Hopkins University and a master's degree in economics from Bocconi University.

Aaditya Mattoo is chief economist of the East Asia and Pacific (EAP) region of the World Bank. He specializes in development, trade, and international cooperation and provides policy advice to governments. Previously, he was the research manager, Trade and International Integration, at the World Bank. Before he joined the World Bank, he was an economic counselor at the World Trade Organization and taught economics at the University of Sussex and Churchill College, Cambridge University. He has published in academic and other journals, and his work has been cited in *The Economist, Financial Times, The New York Times,* and *Time Magazine*. He holds a PhD in economics from the University of Cambridge and an MPhil in economics from the University of Oxford.

Trang Thu Tran is a senior economist in the Economic and Market Research Unit of the International Finance Corporation. Her current research focuses on the role of technology and the private sector in the green transition. Her other research and operational experience spans such topics as firm resilience to shocks; the effects of regulatory reforms; and the design and evaluation of programs to support firms, such as supplier development programs and incentives for technology adoption. She holds a PhD in development economics from the University of Maryland at College Park.

Overview

Abstract

East Asia is helping the rest of the world decarbonize and encouraging the domestic adoption of renewable energy. But there is an imbalance: Even as the region's innovation and investment improve global access to green technologies, the region's own emissions continue to grow, because of the reluctance to penalize carbon-intensive technologies. The disparity between domestic supply and demand also spills over into international trade and is provoking measures limiting access to markets and technologies. Deeper reform of the region's own policies may foster greater international cooperation on climate as well as on innovation and trade in green goods.

Introduction

Countries in East Asia and Pacific (EAP), especially China, are significant emitters of carbon dioxide (CO_2)—and their emissions continue to grow (refer to figure O.1). Progress has been uneven, but the region has committed to gradual decarbonization and improved energy efficiency in recent years (refer to figure O.2). But, as in much of the rest of the world, the current pace of emissions reductions may fail to meet both global climate needs and countries' own commitments. This slow progress is a concern for EAP countries, because they are among the most exposed to the disastrous consequences of climate change.

East Asia and Pacific is decarbonizing—but the current pace likely falls short of meeting climate commitments.

Global greenhouse gas emissions soared in China and doubled in the rest of EAP between 1990 and 2020.

FIGURE 0.1   **CO_2 emissions in China, EAP, the European Union, and the United States, 1990–2020**

GtCO$_2$e

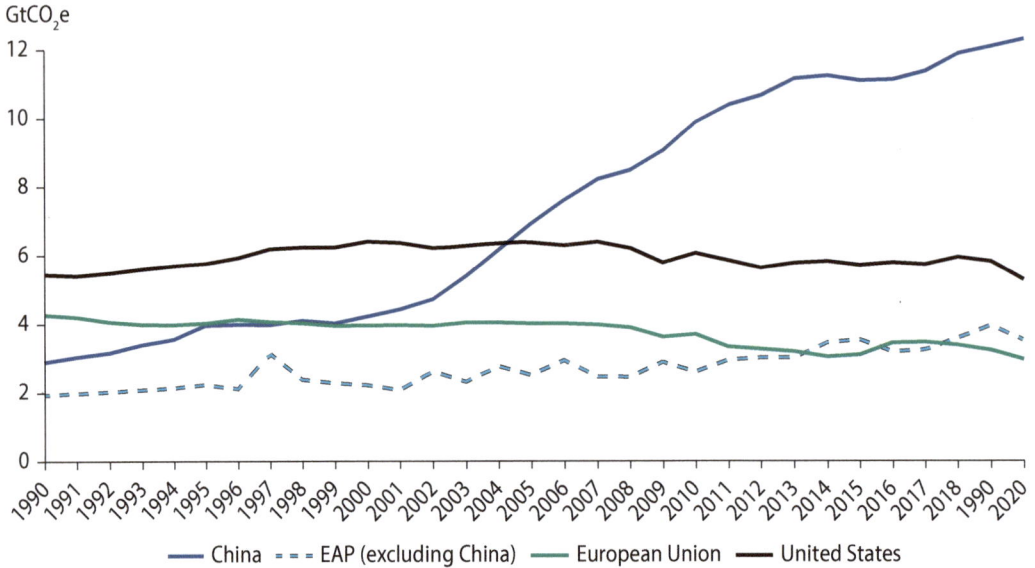

China   — — — EAP (excluding China)   —— European Union   —— United States

Source: Data from Ritchie, Rosado, and Roser 2023.

Note: CO_2 = carbon dioxide; EAP = East Asia and Pacific; GtCO$_2$e = gigatonnes of carbon dioxide equivalent.

Some green technologies (solar, wind energy) are already economically viable; others are likely to be viable only in the near (batteries) or more distant (green hydrogen) future (refer to table O.1 for more examples of technologies at different maturity stages).

Technologies that are currently viable, such as solar photovoltaic (PV) and wind, have seen significant diffusion in Asia, as in other parts of the world. But the pace has differed significantly across countries within the region, with China leading the way and Indonesia among the laggards (refer to figure O.3). This variation reveals the important role the domestic policy environment plays in driving diffusion. For example, differences in state support help explain the contrast between China and the rest of the region in the growth of electric vehicles (EVs).

Whether more ambitious emissions reduction can be achieved without politically unacceptable cuts in consumption or growth will depend on the state and evolution of green technology.

Decarbonization progress within EAP has been uneven.

FIGURE O.2 **Effect of changes in energy intensity and energy mix on emission intensity, selected countries, 1990–2020**

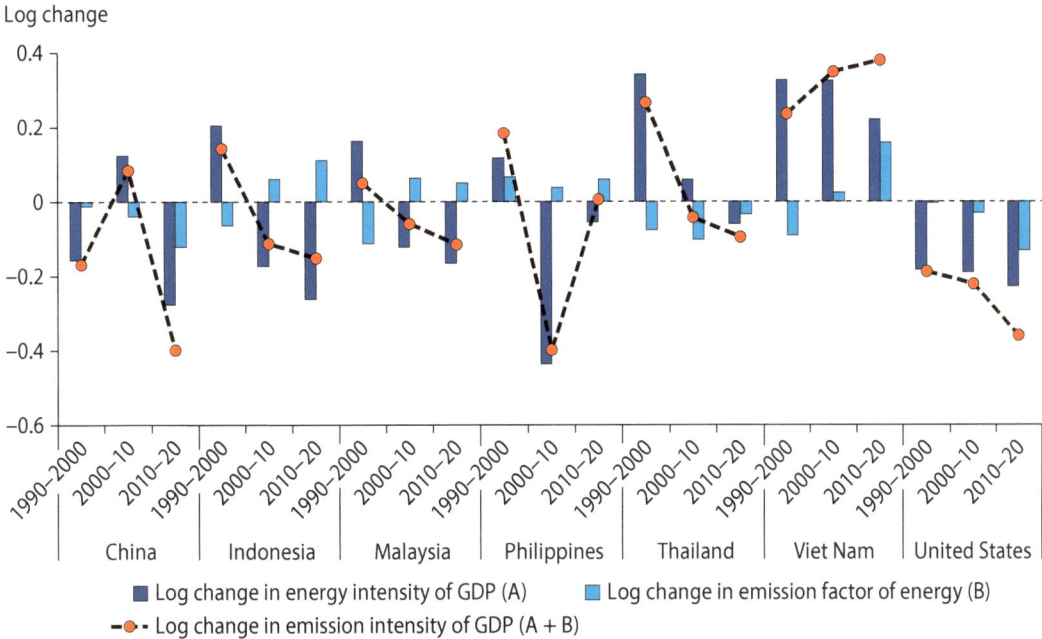

Log change

Log change in energy intensity of GDP (A)   Log change in emission factor of energy (B)
- Log change in emission intensity of GDP (A + B)

Sources: Ritchie, Rosado, and Roser 2023; World Development Indicators (https://databank.worldbank.org/source/world-development -indicators).

Note: EAP = East Asia and Pacific; GDP = gross domestic product.

TABLE O.1 **Emissions contribution and examples of green technologies, by sector**

Sector	Subsector	Total global emissions (%)	Examples of technology	Maturity level
Energy	Electricity/heat	32.0	Solar	Mass market
			Wind plus storage	Mass market for wind, early adoption stage for storage
	Transportation	15.3	Battery electric vehicles	Niche/mass market
			Battery electric trucks	Early adoption stage
			Green ammonia, power-to-liquid fuels	Concept, prototype, or demonstration stage
	Industry	13.1	Green hydrogen-based direct reduction of iron, green ammonia	Concept, prototype, or demonstration stage

(continued)

TABLE O.1   Emissions contribution and examples of green technologies, by sector *(Continued)*

Sector	Subsector	Total global emissions (%)	Examples of technology	Maturity level
	Building	6.3	Heat pumps (residential retrofits)	Niche/mass market
	Other	8.0	Satellite monitoring for large-scale methane leak detection and repairs	Demonstration or early adoption stage
Industrial processes	Industrial processes	6.6	Carbon capture usage and storage, green cement from noncarbonate calcium sources	Concept, prototype, or demonstration stage
Agriculture, forestry, and land use	Agriculture	12.3	Alternative protein	Early adoption stage
			Precision farming	Niche/mass market
	Land-use change and forestry	2.9	Nature-based solutions	Early adoption stage
Waste	Waste	3.5	Pyrolysis treatment for chemically recycling plastics	Concept, prototype, or demonstration stage

Sources: Emissions by sector data are from Climate Watch (https://www.climatewatchdata.org/). Examples of technology options are adapted from IEA (2023) and Systemiq (2023).

Adoption of solar and wind power grew exponentially in several countries between 2000 and 2023.

FIGURE O.3   Adoption of solar and wind power, selected countries, 2000–23

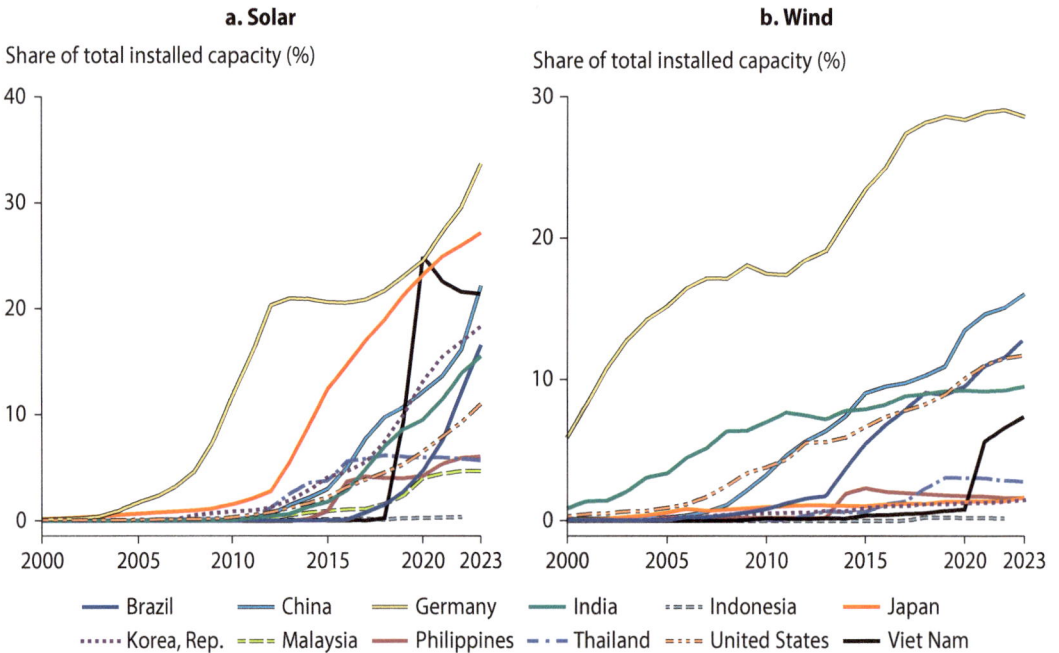

a. Solar

Share of total installed capacity (%)

b. Wind

Share of total installed capacity (%)

Brazil — China — Germany — India — Indonesia — Japan — Korea, Rep. — Malaysia — Philippines — Thailand — United States — Viet Nam

Source: Data from Ember (https://ember-energy.org/data/yearly-electricity-data/).

Policy choices need to be conditioned on a clear understanding of the state of technological development. Where technologies are already viable, policy distortions and market failures prevent their adoption. Eliminating those distortions and remedying those failures would deliver economic benefits (by eliminating the associated deadweight loss) as well as environmental benefits (by addressing the climate externality). These low-hanging win-wins can be grasped unilaterally by a country, provided it can deal with the politically problematic domestic distributional consequences.

Where technologies are not yet viable, economies must decide how far to pursue two costly options: directly encouraging development of the technology or inducing its adoption through a combination of subsidies and taxes that address the knowledge and the environmental externalities (refer to figure O.4).

> **Policy choices need to be informed by the state of technological development.**

FIGURE O.4   Policy framework to support the development and diffusion of green technology

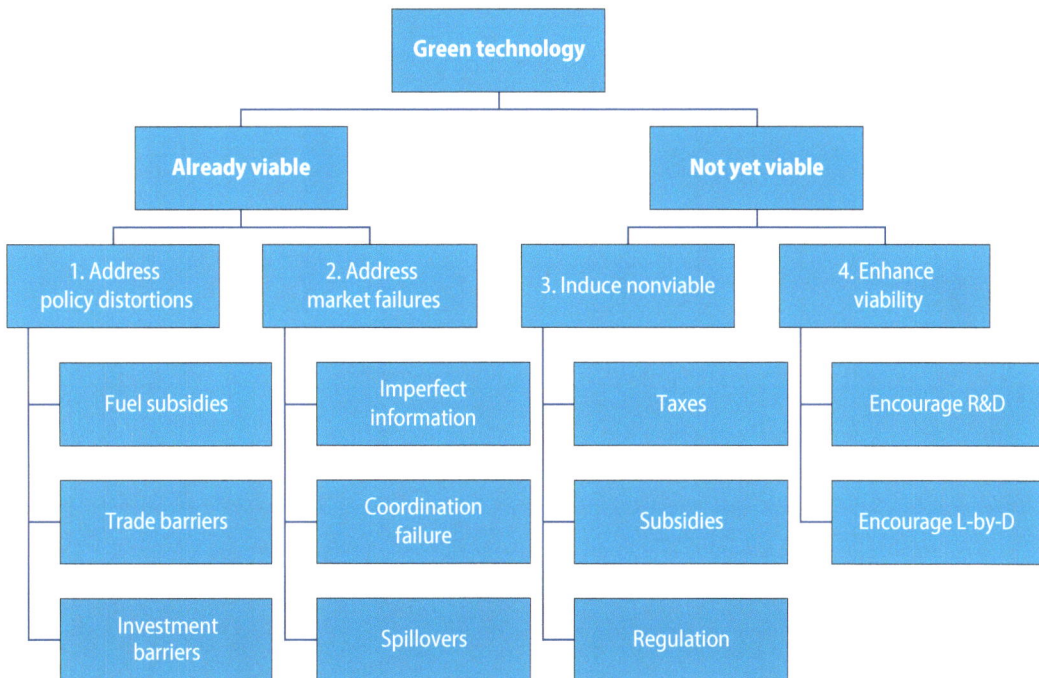

Source: Original figure for this publication.
Note: L-by-D = learning by doing; R&D = research and development.

EAP's progress in green tech development and diffusion

What are EAP countries doing on the four fronts of supporting research and development (R&D), encouraging the adoption of green technology, eliminating policy distortions, and remedying market failure? Countries in the region, especially China, are contributing significantly to the development and global diffusion of green technologies, but they are not doing enough to encourage the adoption of green technologies domestically.

The region's contribution to development and diffusion is felt through innovation, investment, and trade.

China has emerged as a leader in green innovation, with significant support for R&D from the state. China accounts for a significant and growing share of patents in green products, especially in renewable energy and related products and EVs (refer to figure O.5). Its large investments are bringing forward the viability of green technologies by realizing economies of scale and accelerating movements down learning curves in renewable energy and battery storage. The division of labor and high levels of competition across countries in the region—such as Viet Nam in solar panels and Thailand in vehicle components—have also led to significant reductions in costs. China and other EAP countries already occupy a significant share of downstream segments of clean energy supply chains (refer to figure O.6). As a global manufacturing hub, the region is uniquely positioned to harness the green transition to boost its own economic growth.

China has increasingly contributed to the development of new green technologies.

FIGURE O.5   EAP contributions to green patenting, 1995–2020

Green patent applications (thousands)

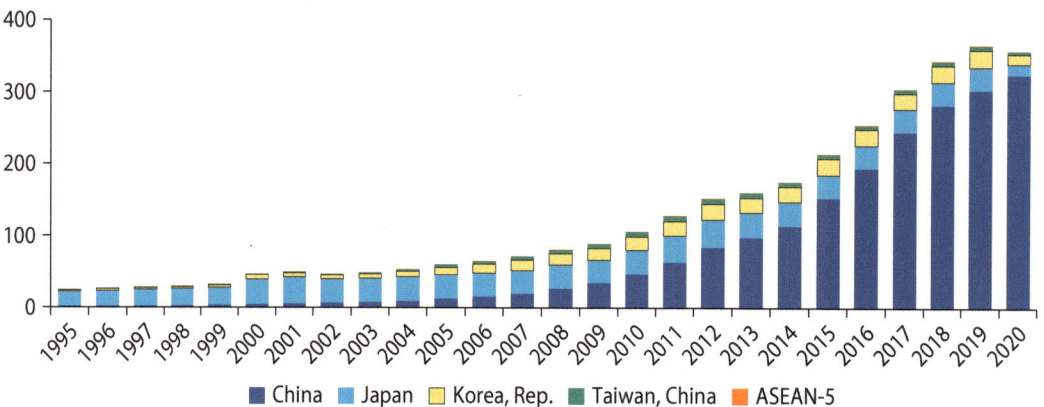

Source: Data from the World Intellectual Property Organization (WIPO) (https://www.wipo.int/en/web/patentscope).
Note: Patents are identified as *green* based on the International Patent Classification (IPC) green inventory of the WIPO. Green patents relate to one of four areas: (1) alternative energy production, such as biofuels and renewables; (2) transportation, including hybrid and electric vehicles, rail vehicles, and marine vessels; (3) energy conservation, including batteries and measurement of electric consumption; and (4) nuclear power generation. ASEAN-5 = Indonesia, Malaysia, the Philippines, Singapore, and Thailand; EAP = East Asia and Pacific.

China dominates downstream segments of clean energy supply chains.

FIGURE O.6   Trade flows of solar PV and EV, by value chain stage, 2016–22

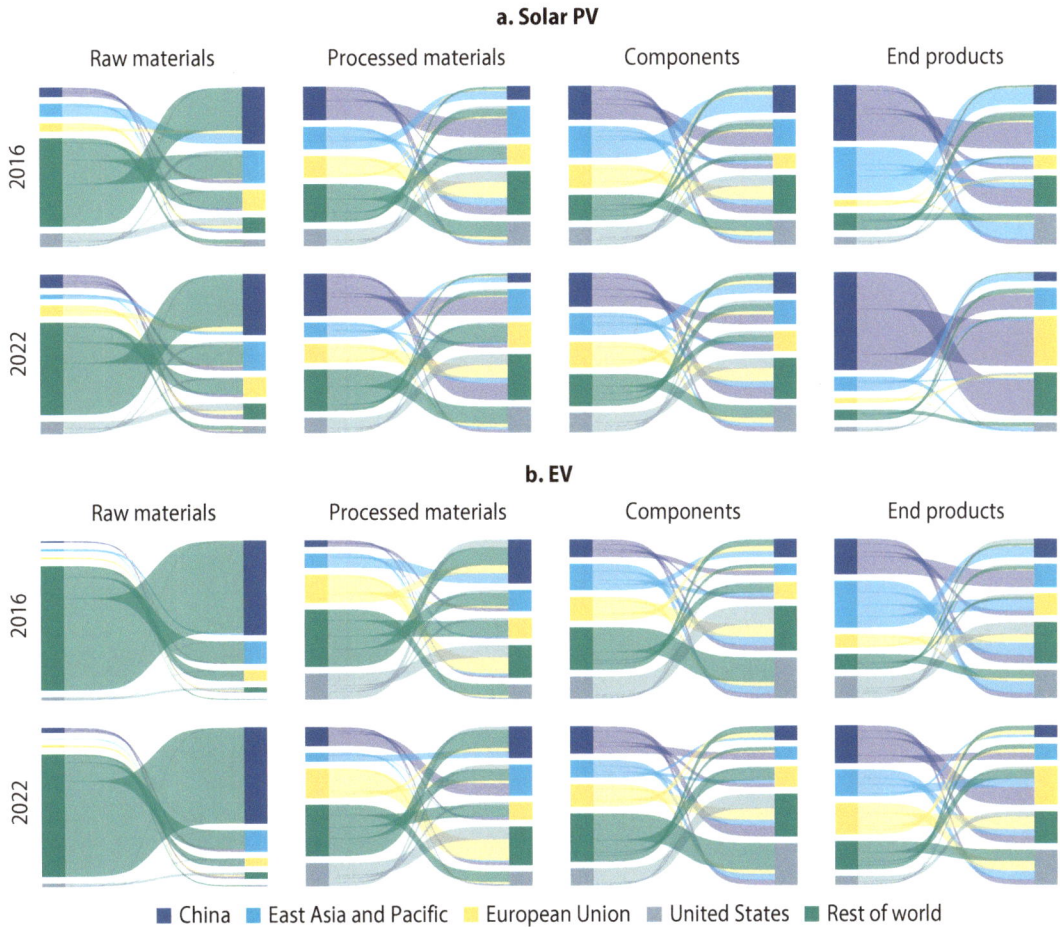

a. Solar PV

b. EV

■ China ■ East Asia and Pacific ■ European Union ■ United States ■ Rest of world

Sources: Bilateral trade data from Base pour l'Analyse du Commerce International (BACI) (https://www.cepii.fr/CEPII/en/bdd_modele/bdd_modele_item.asp?id=37) and classifications in Mealy and Rosenow 2022.
Note: EAP = East Asia and Pacific; EV = electric vehicle; PV = photovoltaic.

Even as the region contributes to the emergence and global spread of green technologies, many developing EAP countries persist with policies—such as subsidies for fossil fuel and tariffs on green products (refer to figure O.7)—that inhibit the domestic deployment of cleaner technologies. And, like much of the rest of the world, most have been reluctant to implement proactive measures like significant carbon taxes to encourage the adoption of green technologies that are not yet viable

Many developing EAP countries continue to maintain policies that inhibit the domestic deployment of cleaner technologies.

(refer to figure O.8). This asymmetry may explain why China's emissions continue to grow and solar- and wind-based generation, despite their unprecedented growth, still accounted for only about 16 percent of total electricity generation in 2023.[1]

> **Tariffs on green goods are relatively high in developing EAP.**

FIGURE O.7 **Average applied tariffs on green goods, selected countries, 2021**

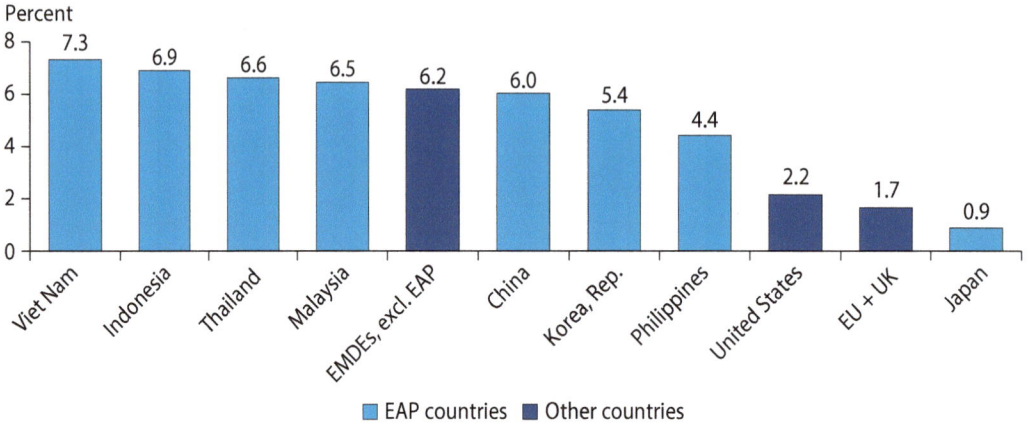

Percent

Viet Nam 7.3, Indonesia 6.9, Thailand 6.6, Malaysia 6.5, EMDEs, excl. EAP 6.2, China 6.0, Korea, Rep. 5.4, Philippines 4.4, United States 2.2, EU + UK 1.7, Japan 0.9

■ EAP countries ■ Other countries

Sources: Data from UN Comtrade Database (https://comtradeplus.un.org/).
Note: The average applied tariffs on green goods are estimated based on data from Comtrade, where green goods are defined as low-carbon technology goods based on Pigato et al. (2020). EAP = East Asia Pacific; EMDEs = emerging market and developing economies; EU = European Union; excl. = excluding; UK = United Kingdom.

> **Different economies have taken different policy approaches to pricing carbon.**

FIGURE O.8 **Effective carbon rates, various countries**

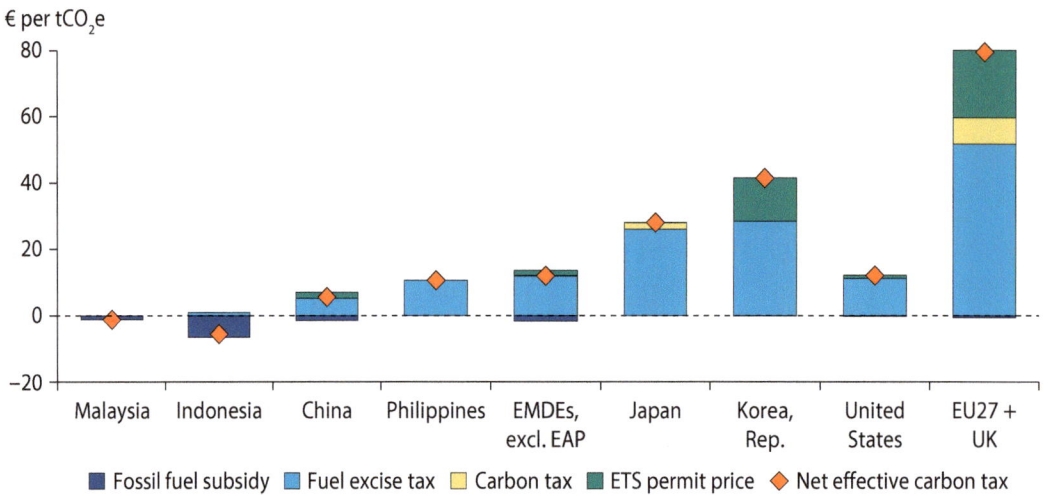

€ per tCO_2e

Malaysia, Indonesia, China, Philippines, EMDEs, excl. EAP, Japan, Korea, Rep., United States, EU27 + UK

■ Fossil fuel subsidy ■ Fuel excise tax ■ Carbon tax ■ ETS permit price ◆ Net effective carbon tax

Source: Data from Organisation for Economic Co-operation and Development, Data Explorer (https://data-explorer.oecd.org/) and The Green Future Index (https://www.technologyreview.com/2023/04/05/1070581/the-green-future-index-2023/).
Note: Net effective carbon tax corresponds to the effective carbon tax (fuel excise tax + ETS permit price + carbon tax) minus the fossil fuel subsidies. Carbon tax refers to all taxes for which the rate is explicitly linked to the fuel's carbon content, irrespective of whether the resulting carbon price is uniform across fuels and uses. EAP = East Asia Pacific; EMDEs = emerging market and developing economies; ETS = emissions trading schemes; EU = European Union; excl. = excluding; tCO_2e = tons of CO_2-equivalent; UK = United Kingdom.

EAP countries have only just begun to remedy failures in markets for green products, especially those arising from imperfect information in capital markets and inadequate coordination in infrastructure and skills. Limited information about investment opportunities and conditions may partly account for the large share of financing cost in the levelized cost of energy in less developed markets (refer to figure O.9). Coordination failures are likely to dampen private investment in shared infrastructure, such as smart grids and charging stations, and in the human capital needed to both produce and use green goods. Given the power sector's central role, grid readiness to accommodate future renewable energy growth is particularly critical. With the exception of China, however, EAP countries continue to lag in investments, system planning, and incentives for renewable energy integration (refer to figure O.10). Apart from concrete measures to facilitate coordination, greater transparency and predictability of policy could shape the expectations of firms and individuals and facilitate investments by reducing at least policy risk.

Market failures and lack of transparent and predictable policies persist.

Simple empirical analysis illustrates how each of these dimensions of policy action and inaction influences the penetration of green technologies like solar PV. Increased viability (reflected in lower relative costs) as well as greater financial and regulatory support boost deployment; higher fossil fuel subsidies and interest rates hurt diffusion (refer to figure O.11). This cross-country pattern illustrates the potential link between green tech diffusion and market and policy drivers. Nevertheless, actual diffusion patterns often follow a nonlinear path and exhibit strong path dependence.

> **Cost of capital accounts for a much higher share of the levelized cost of electricity in less developed markets.**

FIGURE O.9 **Composition of levelized cost of electricity for a utility-scale solar PV plant with final investment decision secured, selected countries, 2021**

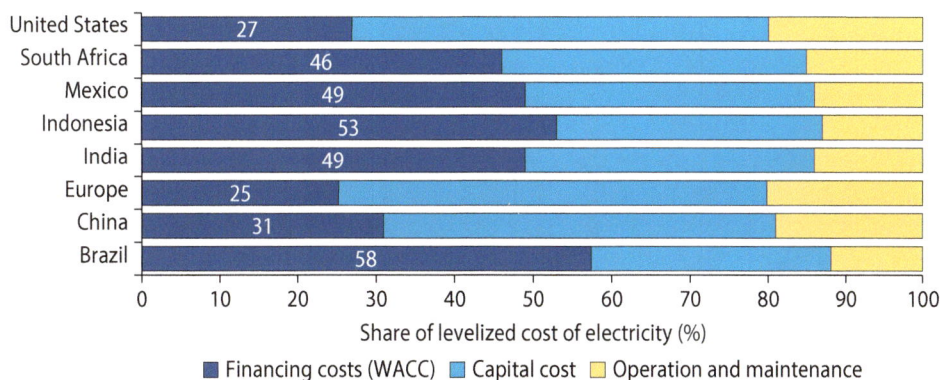

United States: 27
South Africa: 46
Mexico: 49
Indonesia: 53
India: 49
Europe: 25
China: 31
Brazil: 58

Share of levelized cost of electricity (%)

■ Financing costs (WACC) ■ Capital cost ■ Operation and maintenance

Source: International Energy Agency, Cost of Capital Observatory (https://www.iea.org/data-and-statistics/data-tools/cost-of -capital-observatory).
Note: PV = photovoltaic; WACC = weighted average cost of capital (including cost of debt and equity).

China leads the world in renewable energy integration planning and incentives, while other EAP countries lag the rest of the world.

FIGURE O.10   Regulatory score for renewable energy integration planning and incentives, EAP, Europe, and the United States, 2021

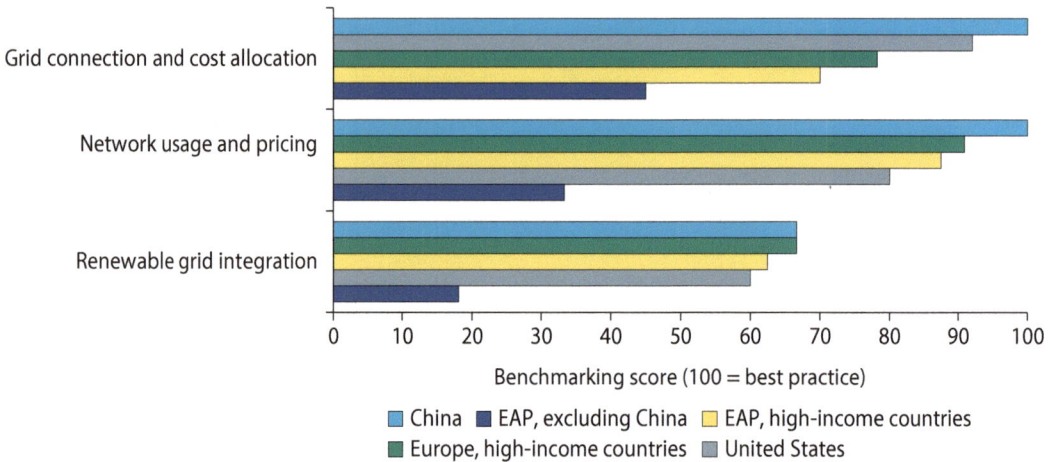

Source: Data from the Regulatory Indicators for Sustainable Energy database (https://rise.esmap.org/scoring-system).
Note: EAP = East Asia and Pacific.

Both cost and policy factors predict the pattern of solar diffusion.

FIGURE O.11   Effect of cost and policy environment on solar PV penetration

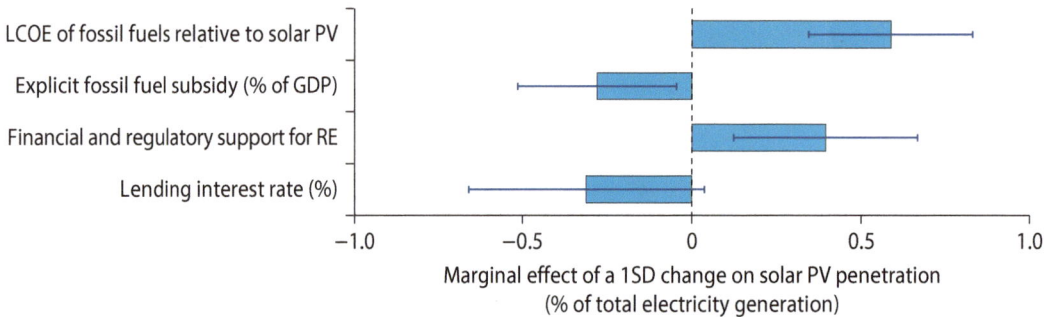

Sources: Data on solar penetration from Ember (https://ember-energy.org/data/yearly-electricity-data/); data on solar practical potential from Solargis (https://globalsolaratlas.info/global-pv-potential-study/); data on LCOE from IRENA (https://www.irena.org/Publications/2024/Sep/Renewable-Power-Generation-Costs-in-2023); data on fossil fuel subsidies from IMF (https://www.imf.org/-/media/Files/Topics/energy-subsidies/EXTERNALfuelsubsidiestemplate2023new.ashx); data on support for renewable energy from World Bank, RISE database (https://www.worldbank.org/en/topic/energy/publication/rise---regulatory-indicators-for-sustainable-energy); data on lending interest rates from World Bank, World Development Indicators (https://databank.worldbank.org/source/world-development-indicators).
Note: Figure shows standardized coefficient estimates from a cross-country regression of solar PV penetration between 2015 and 2022. Other controls include GDP per capita, solar practical potential (the power output achievable by a typical configuration of the utility scale PV system), and year fixed effects. Standard errors (the whiskers) are clustered at the country level and indicate 95 percent confidence intervals. GDP = gross domestic product; IMF = International Monetary Fund; IRENA = International Renewable Energy Agency; LCOE = levelized cost of energy; PV = photovoltaic; RE = renewable energy; SD = standard deviation.

Policy options to promote green technologies

Diffusion of technology can exhibit strong path dependence, especially because the dominance of fossil fuels creates significant inertia. The distinction between economically viable and nonviable technologies is not always clear cut: Learning-by-doing can reduce technology costs, plants take time to build and are slow to depreciate, and complementary inputs may be in short supply. In these circumstances, the optimal policy mix to encourage diffusion is likely to involve a combination of interventions to address market and policy imperfections. Simulation exercises reveal the following:

A combination of interventions is needed to address market and policy imperfections.

- Where existing power purchase agreements offer long-term assured prices for fossil fuel–generated power, limiting the life of such power plants can be useful. Reducing the lifetime of a coal power plant in Indonesia from 40 years to 30 could reduce the long-term bias favoring coal and both the share of coal-generated electricity and emissions by an estimated 10 percent.
- Given the large fixed costs associated with adopting new technologies, as well as the need for synchronized action across interdependent areas (infrastructure, skills), a kick-start through centrally coordinated quantitative targets might help boost diffusion. In Viet Nam, for example, a mandate of a one-time 3.3 percent increase such that the share of solar power generation in 2025 reaches 15 percent could help reduce emissions in the power sector by 292 million metric tons of CO_2 ($MtCO_2$) between 2025 and 2050.
- Prior policy action to remedy policy distortions and market failures is likely to increase the efficacy of fiscal instruments like carbon taxes and subsidies. In Thailand, for example, introducing a carbon tax would raise the solar share to 16 percent from a starting share of 3 percent, but by as much as 54 percent if the initial share were boosted to 15 percent.
- Implementing a policy mix that includes a carbon tax, energy-efficiency regulations, subsidies for renewable energy, and the early phaseout of coal-fired power plants in China could, through learning-by-doing, help lower global solar costs and reduce global emissions by more than 3 percent by 2045.

Where technology is not yet economically viable, countries must consider not only domestic trade-offs but international spillovers. Countries may set their national carbon taxes too low or their subsidies of green production too high in an effort to make domestic firms internationally competitive. In principle, internationally coordinated green technology strategies could yield huge benefits. But in a

International cooperation could help implement globally efficient climate policies; the region—and the rest of the world—cannot count on industrial rivalry to meet climate goals.

world reluctant to tax carbon because of the impact on domestic consumers or firms, climate goals are being advanced by the large subsidies resulting from global green industrial rivalry, which is helping reduce the prices of green goods (refer to figure O.12).

The fact that the region's supply of green goods exceeds the demand for these goods is leading to export surpluses and exacerbating global industrial rivalry. The frictions are provoking restrictions on both the region's exports (such as the antidumping and countervailing actions being contemplated by the European Union and the United States) and its access to vital imports. The former risks depriving the rest of the world of the benefits of cheap green exports from the region; the latter risks slowing the global green innovation engine. For example, US export restrictions and technology licensing requirements have reduced both the quantity and quality of patent output not only of the targeted Chinese firms but also of US firms with Chinese collaborators (refer to figure O.13).

> **Green goods receiving government subsidies are eventually exported at lower prices to other emerging economies.**

FIGURE O.12   Impact of government subsidies on unit cost of green goods, China and rest of world

a. Subsidies from rest of world

b. Subsidies from China

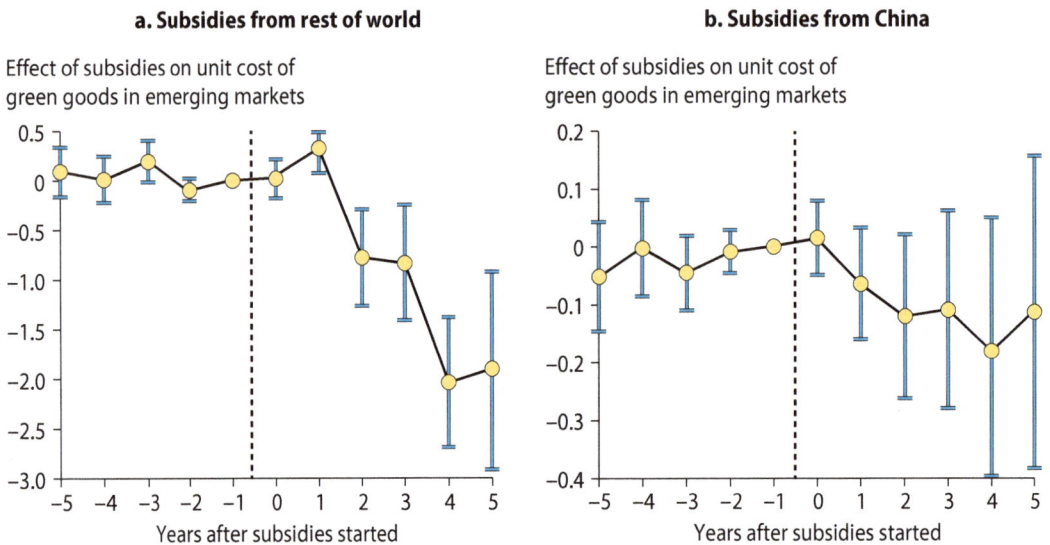

Sources: Bilateral trade flow data from Base pour l'Analyse du Commerce International (BACI) (https://www.cepii.fr/CEPII/en/bdd_modele/bdd_modele_item.asp?id=37); 2012–22 data on subsidies from the Global Trade Alert database (https://globaltradealert.org/).
Note: Figure shows difference-in-differences estimates of the impact of subsidies in exporting countries on import prices in emerging market economies. Panel a shows differences in Chinese export prices of green goods receiving subsidies versus not receiving any subsidies. Panel b shows differences in export prices of green goods receiving subsidies from any countries compared with green goods not receiving any subsidies. Prices were calculated as three-year moving averages. Results are conditional on product (HS6) and year fixed effects. Standard errors are clustered at the HS6 product level; blue vertical lines indicate 95 percent confidence intervals. HS6 = Harmonized System 6.

> Policy restrictions such as the 2018 "China Initiative" may have hurt not only Chinese but also US innovations.

FIGURE O.13 Effect of the 2018 China Initiative on patenting output

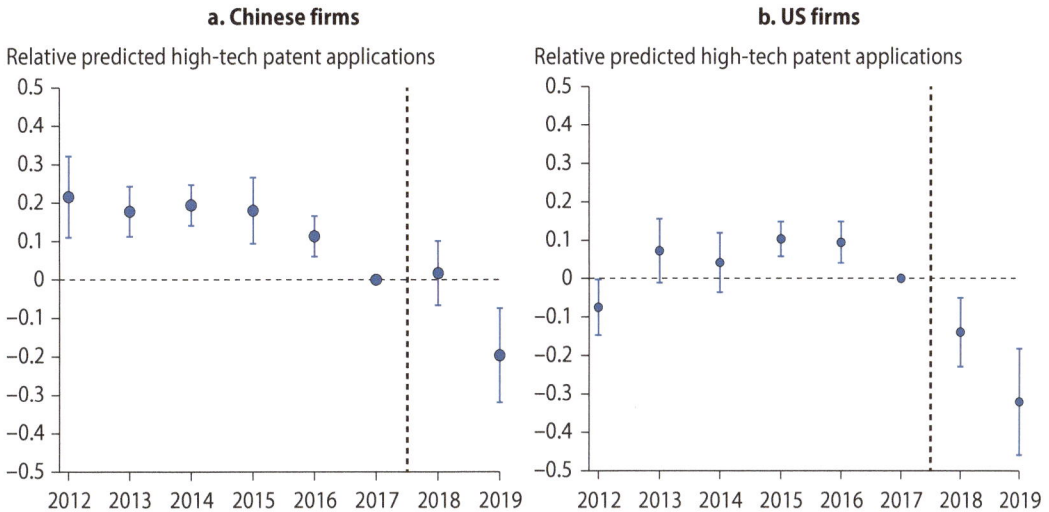

a. Chinese firms

b. US firms

Source: Cao et al. 2024.

Note: Figure shows coefficient estimates with 95 percent confidence interval from an event study on the number of high-tech patent applications worldwide before and after 2018, comparing inventors who had prior collaboration with inventors from China (panel a) and those who collaborated with inventors from the United States (panel b).

Three priorities for policy actions

Measures to encourage the domestic diffusion of cleaner technologies will not only improve the global environment; by boosting domestic demand, they may help also diffuse international tensions.

The analysis in this report suggests three types of policy actions for EAP countries, presented here in order of priority.

> Deeper reform of the region's climate, trade, industrial, and innovation policies can improve domestic diffusion and foster international cooperation.

- *Eliminating distortionary policies*—such as fossil fuel subsidies and barriers to trade and investment—would deliver both economic and environmental benefits. Complementary measures—such as assistance for low-income beneficiaries of fuel subsidies and retraining for workers in fossil fuel industries—would enhance the economic benefits and reduce the political difficulty of reforms.
- Win-wins could also be harvested by *addressing domestic market failures*, such as those arising from imperfections in information (which limit green credit) and coordination (which limit investment in green infrastructure). Remedying such

market imperfections unilaterally will be difficult for small low-income countries, which lack the necessary institutions.

- Going further toward *inducing the adoption of not yet viable technologies*, through carbon taxes or green subsidies, involves incurring an economic cost to secure an environmental benefit. How far EAP countries are willing to go in this respect depends on the commitments they have already made as well as the benefits they receive in return, through emission cuts, assistance, and technology transfers by the rest of the world.

The first two actions unambiguously increase national welfare and can be undertaken unilaterally as soon as the necessary complementary reforms and support are in place. Whether the third improves national welfare depends on what the rest of the world does and therefore can be undertaken at a pace and on a scale determined by past international commitments and future international cooperation. In general, deeper reform of the region's climate, trade, industrial, and innovation policies is likely to foster mutually beneficial international cooperation in each of these areas.

Note

1. Based on data from Ember (https://ember-energy.org/countries-and-regions/china/).

References

Cao, Yu, F. de Nicola, A. Mattoo, and J. Timmis. 2024. "Technological Decoupling? The Impact on Innovation of US Restrictions on Chinese Firms." Policy Research Working Paper 10950, World Bank, Washington, DC. http://hdl.handle.net/10986/42282.

IEA (International Energy Agency). 2023. *Energy Technology Guide 2023*. Paris.

Pigato, M., S. J. Black, D. Dussaux, Z. Mao, M. McKenna, R. Rafaty, and S. Touboul. 2020. *Technology Transfer and Innovation for Low-Carbon Development*. International Development in Focus. Washington, DC: World Bank. https://doi.org/10.1596/978-1-4648-1500-3.

Ritchie, H., P. Rosado, and M. Roser. 2023. "CO_2 and Greenhouse Gas Emissions." https://ourworldindata.org/co2-and-greenhouse-gas-emissions.

Rosenow, S. K., and P. A. Mealy. 2024. "Turning Risks into Rewards: Diversifying the Global Value Chains of Decarbonization Technologies." Policy Research Working Paper 10696, World Bank, Washington, DC.

Systemiq. 2023. *The Breakthrough Effect: How to Trigger a Cascade of Tipping Points to Accelerate the Net Zero Transition*. London: Sytemiq. https://www.systemiq.earth/wp-content/uploads/2023/01/The-Breakthrough-Effect.pdf.

Abbreviations

AFOLU	agriculture, forestry, and other land use
BEV	battery electric vehicle
BF-BOF	blast furnace–basic oxygen furnace
CCMT	climate change mitigation technology
CCS	carbon capture and sequestration
CDR	carbon dioxide removal
CO_2	carbon dioxide
EAF	electric arc furnace
EAP	East Asia and Pacific
EMDEs	emerging market and developing economies
ETS	emissions trading scheme
EV	electric vehicle
FDI	foreign direct investment
FiT	feed-in tariff
FTT	Future Technology Transformation (model)
GDP	gross domestic product
Gt	gigaton (1 billion tonnes)
$GtCO_2$	gigatons (1 billion tonnes) of CO_2
ICE	internal combustion engine
IEA	International Energy Agency
IP	intellectual property
IPCC	Intergovernmental Panel on Climate Change

IPRs	intellectual property rights
IRA	Inflation Reduction Act of 2022 (United States)
$ktCO_2e$	kilotons (1,000 tonnes) of carbon dioxide equivalent
kWh	kilowatt-hour
LCOE	levelized cost of energy/electricity
LCR	local content requirement
LCT	low-carbon technology
LPG	liquefied petroleum gas
$MtCO_2$	megatons (1 million tonnes) of carbon dioxide
MW	megawatt(s)
NDC	Nationally Determined Contribution
NTB	nontariff barrier
NZE	net-zero carbon emissions
OECD	Organisation for Economic Co-operation and Development
PV	photovoltaic
R&D	research and development
S$	Singapore dollar
tCO_2	tons of carbon dioxide
TEPA	Taiwanese Environmental Protection Administration
₩	Korean won
¥	Japanese yen

Note: Unless otherwise indicated, all monetary units are in US dollars (US$).

Introduction | 1

Decarbonization trends in East Asia and Pacific

East Asia's approach to climate change mitigation will have an outsize impact on the world's progress toward its climate goal, because the region's carbon footprint is large and increasing (World Bank 2022a, 2022b, 2022c, 2023a, 2023b). Historically, Western economies were the primary contributors to the stock of atmospheric greenhouse gas emissions. Their contribution is now in decline (UNEP 2023). Conversely, developing East Asia has become a significant emitter. China is now the world's largest emitter, responsible for 30 percent of global emissions annually, and its emissions continue to rise. The rest of developing East Asia and Pacific (EAP) nearly doubled its emissions between 1990 and 2020 (refer to figure 1.1), producing almost 10 percent of the global total by 2020.

The pace at which developing East Asia decarbonizes matters profoundly for the global climate.

The ongoing rise in emissions exacerbates the gap between current trajectories and the targets set in the Paris Agreement, which aim to limit global warming to well below 2°C and pursue efforts to stay under 1.5°C. According to the latest report by the United Nations Environment Programme (UNEP 2023), the carbon budget—the total amount of carbon that can be emitted for temperatures to stay below a given limit—is dwindling: By 2023, only about 250 gigatonnes of carbon dioxide ($GtCO_2$), or roughly six years of current emissions, remain before the likelihood of exceeding 1.5°C warming reaches 50 percent.[1] The actions taken in this decade will determine whether the long-term temperature goals of the Paris Agreement are attainable.

> **Global greenhouse gas emissions soared in China and doubled in the rest of EAP between 1990 and 2020.**

FIGURE 1.1   **CO_2 emissions in China, EAP, the European Union, and the United States, 1990–2020**

GtCO$_2$e

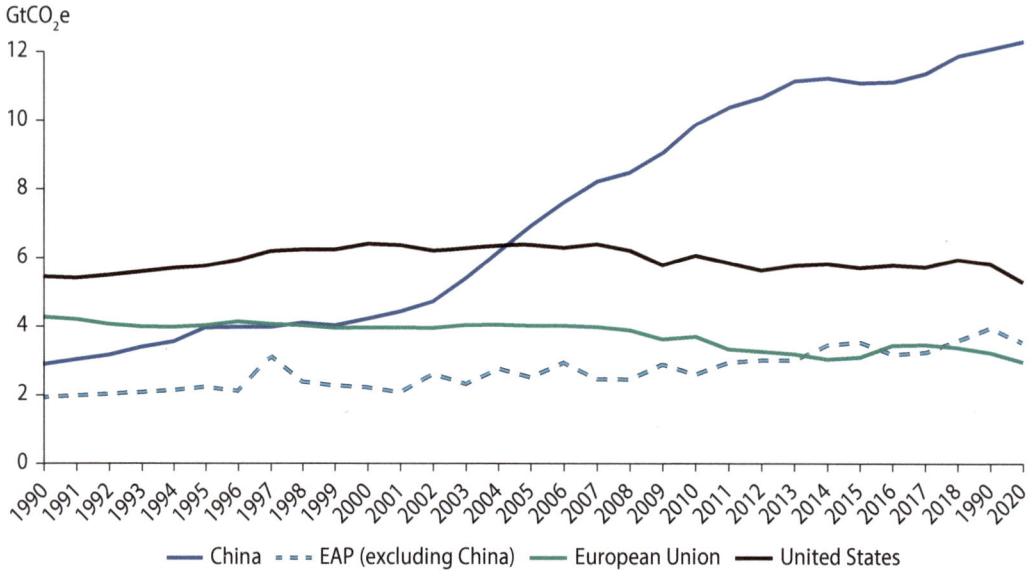

Source: Data from Ritchie, Rosado, and Roser 2023.
Note: CO_2 = carbon dioxide; EAP = East Asia and Pacific; GtCO$_2$e = gigatonnes of carbon dioxide equivalent.

Despite some progress, East Asian economies, driven by China, are still significantly more carbon-intensive than the world's average. Global emission intensity—measured as CO_2 produced per unit of gross domestic product (GDP)—declined over the last 30 years, driven by the steady fall in high-income countries. Carbon intensity also declined in Asia, but the decline was much more modest (refer to figure 1.2).

Progress toward decarbonization has been uneven. Carbon intensity in most economies in the EAP region has declined, thanks to improved energy efficiency. This progress, however, has been partially offset by countries such as Indonesia and the Philippines, whose energy mix has become dirtier (refer to figure 1.3). Viet Nam stands out: Its carbon intensity is still increasing, and energy efficiency has not improved in the past decades. China has seen the biggest improvement in emission intensity, but the enormous growth in its total emissions suggests that output growth fueled by dirty sources far outpaced the economy's decarbonization process. This experience underscores the challenges of limiting emissions while pursuing economic growth.

China's carbon intensity far exceeds the global average, while the rest of EAP struggles to improve.

FIGURE 1.2   Carbon intensity in China, EAP, the European Union, the United States, and the world, 1990–2018

Emission intensity (kgCO$_2$ per US$)

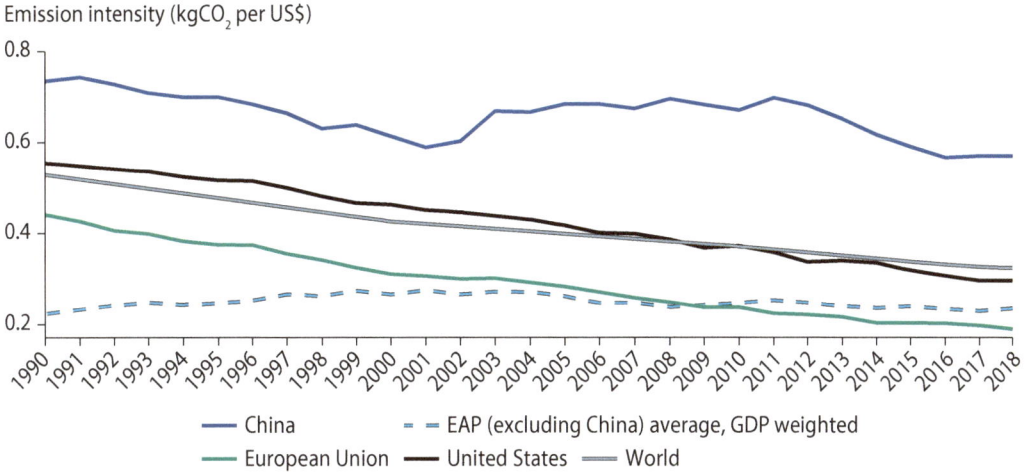

Legend: China; EAP (excluding China) average, GDP weighted; European Union; United States; World

Source: Ritchie, Rosado, and Roser 2023.
Note: EAP = East Asia and Pacific; GDP = gross domestic product; kgCO$_2$ = kilograms of carbon dioxide.

Decarbonization progress within EAP has been uneven.

FIGURE 1.3   Contribution to changes in emission intensity in select EAP countries and the United States, 1990–2020

Log change

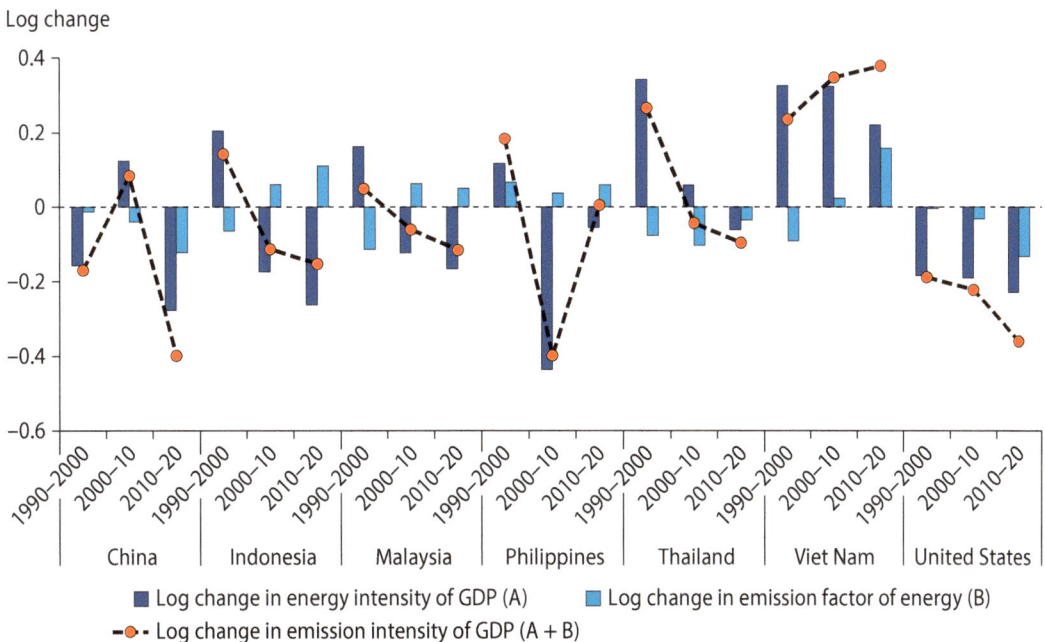

Legend: Log change in energy intensity of GDP (A); Log change in emission factor of energy (B); Log change in emission intensity of GDP (A + B)

Sources: Ritchie, Rosado, and Roser 2023; World Development Indicators (https://databank.worldbank.org/source/world-development-indicators).
Note: EAP = East Asia and Pacific; GDP = gross domestic product.

The importance of technology in achieving the net-zero emission goals

Firm-level evidence suggests that technological change, rather than changes in the composition of economic activities, is a potential driver of decarbonization progress in EAP. A decomposition analysis of Indonesian manufacturing firm–level data shows that production is becoming more energy efficient over time, partly mitigating the emission impact of increased output and an increasingly polluting fuel mix (refer to figure 1.4). These gains in energy efficiency are not the result of shifts in the manufacturing sector's composition. They are observed within individual sectors, including more narrowly defined ones. This trend in sectoral energy efficiency—often termed the *technique effect*—points to the role that changing technology plays in driving down emission intensity.

> **Technology is critical to achieving the net-zero emission goals.**

Technological change has facilitated the transition to a lower-carbon economy. But a much faster pace than historical trends is required to meet climate targets (IPCC 2023). Achieving net-zero carbon emissions (NZE) requires a radical reduction of net anthropogenic CO_2 emissions from current levels, which were just under 37 Gt in 2022.[2]

Most technologies needed to meet this goal by 2070 are not yet mature. About 35 percent of emissions are expected to come from technologies still in the prototype or demonstration stages; another 40 percent will come from technologies that are still in the early adoption stage (IEA 2020). Model simulations by the International Energy Agency (IEA) suggest that behavioral changes—such as reducing excessive or wasteful energy use and switching transport modes—play only a marginal role in the annual CO_2 emissions saving needed to achieve NZE. Getting to NZE will require both the rapid deployment of already available technology solutions and the development of new technologies (refer to box 1.1 for examples of green technologies at varying maturity levels).

Technological change within sectors helped reduce energy intensity, but an increasingly carbon-intensive fuel mix hampers progress on emission reduction in Indonesia.

FIGURE 1.4 **Contribution to changes in emission intensity, Indonesia manufacturing, 1991–2017**

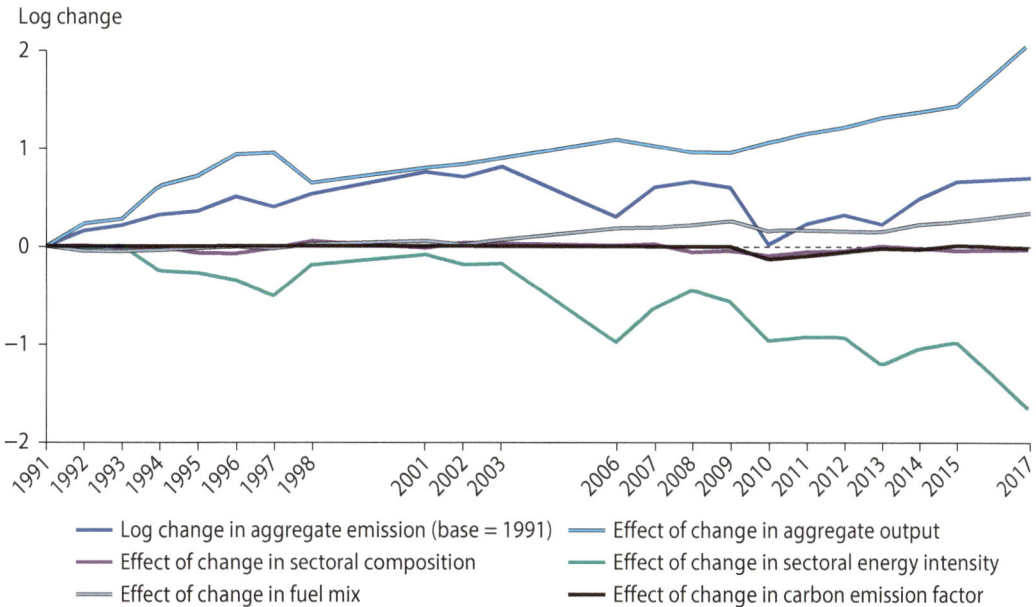

Source: Data from the Manufacturing Survey of Large and Medium-Sized Firms in Indonesia (Statistik Industri).
Note: Figure shows results of a Log Mean Divisia Index decomposition. Sectors are two-digit International Standard Industrial Classification (ISIC) sectors. Results are broadly similar with three-digit and four-digit sectors. Data exclude 1999, 2000, 2004, and 2005 because of potential measurement errors; data for 2016 were not available.

Box 1.1. What technology options exist for deeper decarbonization?

This report defines green technologies as climate change mitigation technologies (CCMTs). The goal of mitigation is to preserve a biosphere that can sustain human civilization and the range of ecosystem services that surround and support it by reducing anthropogenic greenhouse emissions to limit warming based on the global goals agreed to in the Paris Agreement (IPCC 2023).

CCMT encompasses technologies that reduce the sources or enhance the sinks of greenhouse gases. Technologies to help limit emissions involve improving energy efficiency, transitioning to renewable energy sources, promoting electrification, adopting more sustainable transportation methods, and changing land-use practices, among other strategies. Any remaining emissions—those that are difficult to eliminate—will need to be balanced with carbon removal methods. Table B1.1.1 provides examples of technology options by sector.

(continued)

Box 1.1.   What technology options exist for deeper decarbonization?
(Continued)

TABLE B1.1.1   **Emissions contribution and examples of green technologies, by sector**

Sector	Subsector	Total global emissions (%)	Examples of technology	Maturity level
Energy	Electricity/heat	32.0	Solar	Mass market
			Wind plus storage	Mass market for wind, early adoption stage for storage
	Transportation	15.3	Battery electric vehicles	Niche/mass market
			Battery electric trucks	Early adoption stage
			Green ammonia, power-to-liquid fuels	Concept, prototype, or demonstration stage
	Industry	13.1	Green hydrogen-based direct reduction of iron, green ammonia	Concept, prototype, or demonstration stage
	Building	6.3	Heat pumps (residential retrofits)	Niche/mass market
	Other	8.0	Satellite monitoring for large-scale methane leak detection and repairs	Demonstration or early adoption stage
Industrial processes	Industrial processes	6.6	Carbon capture usage and storage, green cement from noncarbonate calcium sources	Concept, prototype, or demonstration stage
Agriculture, forestry, and land use	Agriculture	12.3	Alternative protein	Early adoption stage
			Precision farming	Niche/mass market
	Land-use change and forestry	2.9	Nature-based solutions	Early adoption stage
Waste	Waste	3.5	Pyrolysis treatment for chemically recycling plastics	Concept, prototype, or demonstration stage

Sources: Emissions by sector data are from Climate Watch. Examples of technology options are adapted from IEA (2023) and Systemiq (2023).

(continued)

Box 1.1.   What technology options exist for deeper decarbonization?
    (Continued)

These technologies exist on a spectrum, from those that have been widely adopted to those that are still at the concept stage:

- In the energy sector, more mature technologies, such as renewable energy, especially solar and wind, have seen remarkable cost reductions and widespread deployment. The dynamics for solar photovoltaic (PV) are the most impressive: Their cost fell by a factor of 10,000 between the first commercial application on a satellite in 1958 and the signing of power purchase agreements in 2019 (IPCC 2023). Solar energy also has the greatest technical potential of all renewable sources, far exceeding global energy needs for even the most ambitious mitigation scenarios. The Earth receives about 120,000 terawatts of solar energy—nearly 10,000 times global consumption. After accounting for land-use constraints, solar PV's technical potential remains around 300 petawatt-hours per year, nearly twice current electricity use. Its adoption is limited not by resource availability but by grid integration and market conditions.

- Battery electric vehicles (BEVs) represent another widely adopted technology. They are considered crucial for tackling emissions in the transport sector. BEVs exemplify the efficiency gain from electrification: They convert over 85–90 percent of the electrical energy from the battery. Internal combustion engine (ICE) vehicles are much less efficient, typically converting only about 20–30 percent of the energy from fuel sources. Where applicable, BEVs further reduce emissions through their reliance on electricity, which is becoming increasingly cleaner. By some estimates, BEVs can cut lifecycle emissions by about two-thirds compared with ICE cars in Europe. As electricity generation becomes cleaner, the benefits of BEVs are expected to grow (CarbonBrief 2023).

- Technologies to decarbonize heavy industries are significantly less mature. About 42 percent of these emissions—about 10 percent of global emissions—come from combustion to produce large amounts of high-temperature heat for industrial products like cement, steel, and petrochemicals. Electrification and fuel switching to lower-emitting sources are one of the strategies to decarbonize this demand for industrial heat. "Green hydrogen"—made via electrolysis, using electricity to separate hydrogen from water—is considered a promising alternative fuel. It is currently cheaper to capture and bury CO_2 from these processes than it is to switch out systems for low-carbon alternatives, however.

(continued)

Box 1.1.   What technology options exist for deeper decarbonization?
(Continued)

• More speculative technologies, such as geoengineering solutions, have been proposed to avert the effects of climate change by removing CO_2 from the atmosphere (carbon dioxide removal [CDR]) or directly modifying the Earth's energy balance at a large scale (solar radiation modification). CDR technologies include ocean iron fertilization, enhanced weathering, ocean alkalinization, and direct air carbon capture and storage. CDR technologies could potentially draw down atmospheric CO_2 faster than the Earth's natural carbon cycle and reduce reliance on biomass-based removal. However, these technologies are still nascent. The biggest direct air carbon plant in the world has an annual capacity of 4,000 tons, equivalent to just a few seconds of total global emissions (Ma 2024).

Source: This box draws heavily on IPCC (2023).

Policy framework for green technology development and diffusion

This report proposes a framework to guide policy decisions based on the (local) viability of technologies for users (refer to figure 1.5). The framework considers not only the technical maturity of technologies—as indicated by frameworks such as the technology readiness level assessment (IEA, n.d.)—but also barriers to their adoption in a specific region or country context. A technology that is cost-competitive globally may not be viable locally because of differences in factor endowments or industrial structure. Viability—defined as cost-competitiveness relative to the existing technology—will determine which policies are appropriate to encourage the adoption or development of green technologies. When green technologies are viable, removing policy and market distortions that hinder their adoption will facilitate diffusion. For technologies that are not yet viable, diffusion requires policies to internalize the negative externalities of dirty technologies and encourage investments to bring down the cost—absolute or relative—of green technologies.

The book is organized as follows. Chapter 2 briefly surveys the state of green technologies. Chapter 3 examines the EAP region's role in accelerating the global development and diffusion of green technologies. Chapter 4 focuses on the diffusion of green technologies in the region and factors that could promote or inhibit their diffusion. Chapter 5 reviews the policy landscape and outlines actions to facilitate the region's transition to green technologies. Chapter 6 provides considerations for policy making.

Policy choices need to be informed by the state of technological development.

FIGURE 1.5   **Policy framework to support the development and diffusion of green technology**

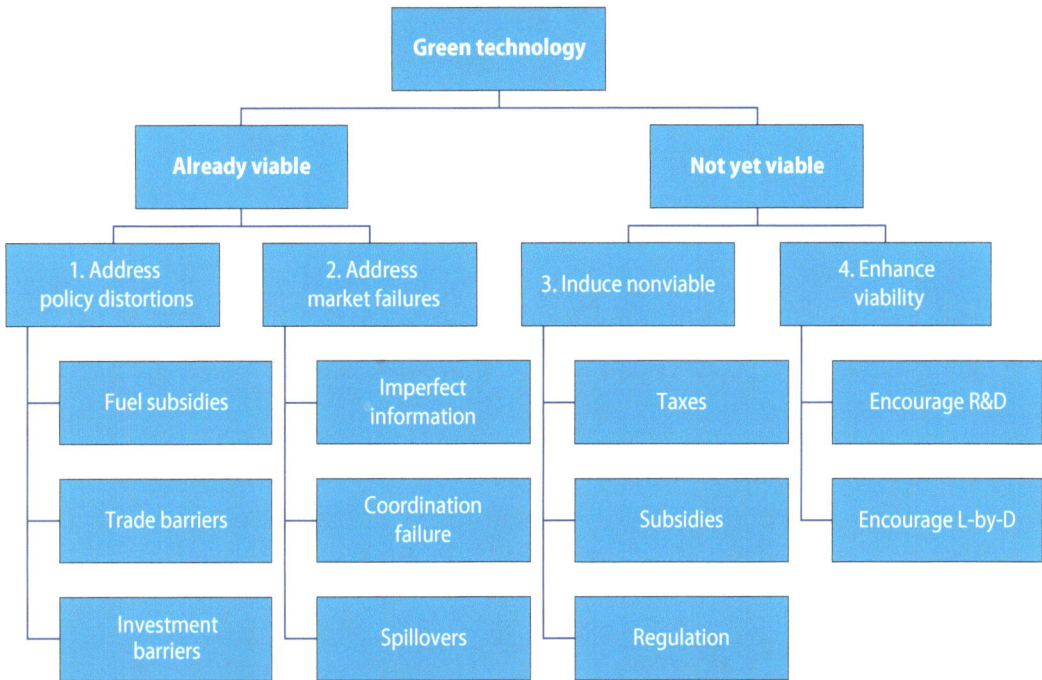

Source: Original figure for this publication.
Note: L-by-D = learning-by-doing; R&D = research and development.

Notes

1. Global warming is almost proportional to the total net amount of CO_2 cumulatively emitted as a result of human activities. Limiting global warming to a specified level therefore requires that the total amount of CO_2 emissions ever emitted be kept within a finite carbon budget (Fankhauser et al. 2022).

2. The concept of NZE applies to timescales beyond decades and generally refers to CO_2 emissions, given their longevity in the atmosphere (other greenhouse gases typically have shorter atmospheric lifespans). Non-CO_2 anthropogenic warming is therefore better determined not by cumulative emissions but by the current emission rate plus a small correction for the long-term climate response (Fankhauser et al. 2022).

References

CarbonBrief. 2023. "Factcheck: 21 Misleading Myths about Electric Vehicles." October 24. https://www.carbonbrief.org/factcheck-21-misleading-myths-about-electric-vehicles/.

Fankhauser, S., S. M. Smith, M. Allen, K. Axelsson, T. Hale, C. Hepburn, J. M. Kendall, R. Khosla, J. Lezaun, E. Mitchell-Larson, M. Obersteiner, L. Rajamani, R. Rickaby,

N. Seddon, and T. Wetzer. 2022. "The Meaning of Net Zero and How to Get It Right." *Nature Climate Change* 12 (1): 15–21. https://doi.org/10.1038/s41558-021-01245-w.

IEA (International Energy Agency). n.d. *Innovation*. Paris: IEA. https://www.iea.org/energy-system/decarbonisation-enablers/innovation.

IEA (International Energy Agency). 2020. *Clean Energy Innovation*. Paris: IEA. https://www.iea.org/reports/clean-energy-innovation.

IEA (International Energy Agency). 2023. *Energy Technology Perspectives 2023*. Paris: IEA. https://www.iea.org/reports/energy-technology-perspectives-2023.

IPCC (Intergovernmental Panel on Climate Change). 2023. *Climate Change 2022: Mitigation of Climate Change*. Working Group III contribution to the Sixth Assessment Report of the Intergovernmental Panel on Climate Change. Cambridge, UK: Cambridge University Press.

Ma, M. 2024. "Sergey Brin-Backed Carbon Removal Startup Nears Firing Up Its New Plant." Bloomberg. April 20, 2024. https://www.bloomberg.com/news/articles/2024-04-29/startup-prepares-new-oregon-carbon-dioxide-removal-plant-for-operations.

Ritchie, H., P. Rosado, and M. Roser. 2023. "CO_2 and Greenhouse Gas Emissions." Published online at OurWorldinData.org. https://ourworldindata.org/co2-and-greenhouse-gas-emissions.

Systemiq. 2023. *The Breakthrough Effect: How to Trigger a Cascade of Tipping Points to Accelerate the Net Zero Transition*. London: Sytemiq. https://www.systemiq.earth/wp-content/uploads/2023/01/The-Breakthrough-Effect.pdf.

UNEP (United Nations Environment Programme). 2023. *Emissions Gap Report 2023: Broken Record*. Nairobi: UNEP. https://www.unep.org/interactives/emissions-gap-report/2023/.

World Bank. 2022a. *China Country Climate and Development Report*. Washington, DC: World Bank. https://hdl.handle.net/10986/38136.

World Bank. 2022b. *Philippines Country Climate and Development Report*. Washington, DC: World Bank. https://hdl.handle.net/10986/38280.

World Bank. 2022c. *Vietnam Country Climate and Development Report*. Washington, DC: World Bank. https://hdl.handle.net/10986/37618.

World Bank. 2023a. *Cambodia Country Climate and Development Report*. Washington, DC: World Bank. https://doi.org/10.1596/40467.

World Bank. 2023b. *Indonesia Country Climate and Development Report*. Washington, DC: World Bank. https://doi.org/10.1596/39750.

Which green technologies are already viable? | 2

The current cost of green technologies

The state and evolution of green technology will determine whether more ambitious emissions reduction can be achieved without politically unacceptable cuts in consumption or growth. This chapter examines the viability of different green technologies. Some (solar, wind energy) are already viable; others are likely to be viable only in the near (batteries) or more distant future (green hydrogen). Much will depend on the pace of learning-by-doing.

Perhaps the best-known headline about green technologies today is the progress the world has made in bringing down the cost of renewable energy. Between 2010 and 2022, the cost of solar power fell by 89 percent, and the cost of offshore wind power fell by 59 percent (IRENA 2023). The decline in prices has made unit generation costs cheaper from renewables than from fossil fuels in many parts of the world. Since 2021, the average levelized cost of energy (LCOE) of both solar and offshore wind has been lower than that of coal and gas (refer to figure 2.1).[1]

> The cost of specific technologies has fallen dramatically, but the relative cost and scope for emissions reduction of green technologies still varies widely.

Renewable technologies such as solar and wind also have substantial scope to reduce net emissions (IPCC 2023 and figure 2.2). Renewables are not yet perfect substitutes for fossil fuels, however, because of their intermittent nature, leading to a greater need for redundancy at higher levels of penetration (refer to figure 2.2 for the estimates by the Intergovernmental Panel on Climate Change [IPCC] of cost increases at higher levels of emission reductions). Their higher penetration requires complementary technologies, such as energy storage. The falling cost of energy

---

Solar and offshore wind are now cheaper than coal and gas.

FIGURE 2.1   LCOE premium for solar PV and offshore wind, 2012–22

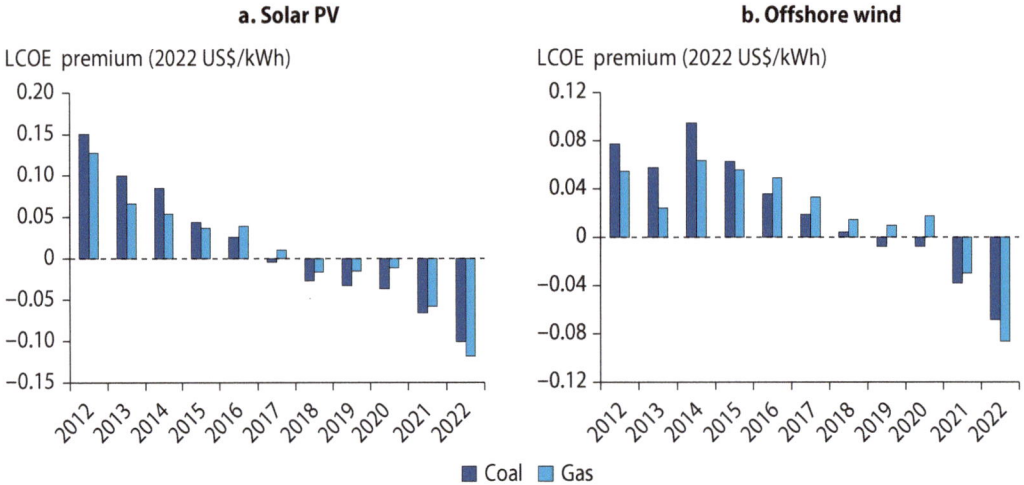

a. Solar PV

LCOE premium (2022 US$/kWh)

b. Offshore wind

LCOE premium (2022 US$/kWh)

■ Coal ■ Gas

Source: Data from the International Renewable Energy Agency's Renewable Generation Cost database (https://www.irena.org /Publications/2023/Aug/Renewable-Power-Generation-Costs-in-2022).
Note: The LCOE masks significant differences across countries. Within the East Asia and Pacific region, for example, the average LCOE for solar PV ranged from US$0.30/kWh) in China to US$0.76/kWh in Viet Nam in 2022. The premium is the difference between the average LCOE for coal and gas electricity generation projects across 20 countries and the global weighted-average LCOE from newly commissioned solar PV and offshore wind power. kWh = kilowatt-hour; LCOE = levelized cost of energy; PV = photovoltaic.

storage technologies holds the potential to improve the viability of renewables: Between 2010 and 2024, the LCOE for lithium-ion batteries fell a whopping 90 percent (IEA 2024).

Beyond the energy sector, many currently cost-competitive technology options cover a smaller amount of the carbon dioxide (CO_2) reduction potential. These technologies largely involve increasing energy efficiency or reducing energy demand in the buildings and transport sectors—by, for example, adopting low-energy lighting and shifting to public transportation.

The relative costs of green technologies in industry and in agriculture, forestry, and other land use (AFOLU) illustrate the difficulty of reducing emissions in these harder-to-abate sectors, which together account for 66 percent of total direct emissions (IPCC 2023). The technology options for reducing emissions in these sectors are more expensive than their dirty alternatives. A rough estimate based on figure 2.2 (which does not adjust for overlaps) suggests that cost-competitive technologies cover less than a fifth of the emissions reduction potential. The remaining potential has to rely on technologies that are not yet economically viable.

Green technologies vary widely in relative cost and mitigation potential.

FIGURE 2.2   Overview of mitigation options and their estimated ranges of costs and potentials in 2030 (IPCC Sixth Assessment Report, figure SPM.7)

Many options available now in all sectors are estimated to offer substantial potential to reduce net emissions by 2030. Relative potentials and costs will vary across countries and in the longer term compared to 2030.

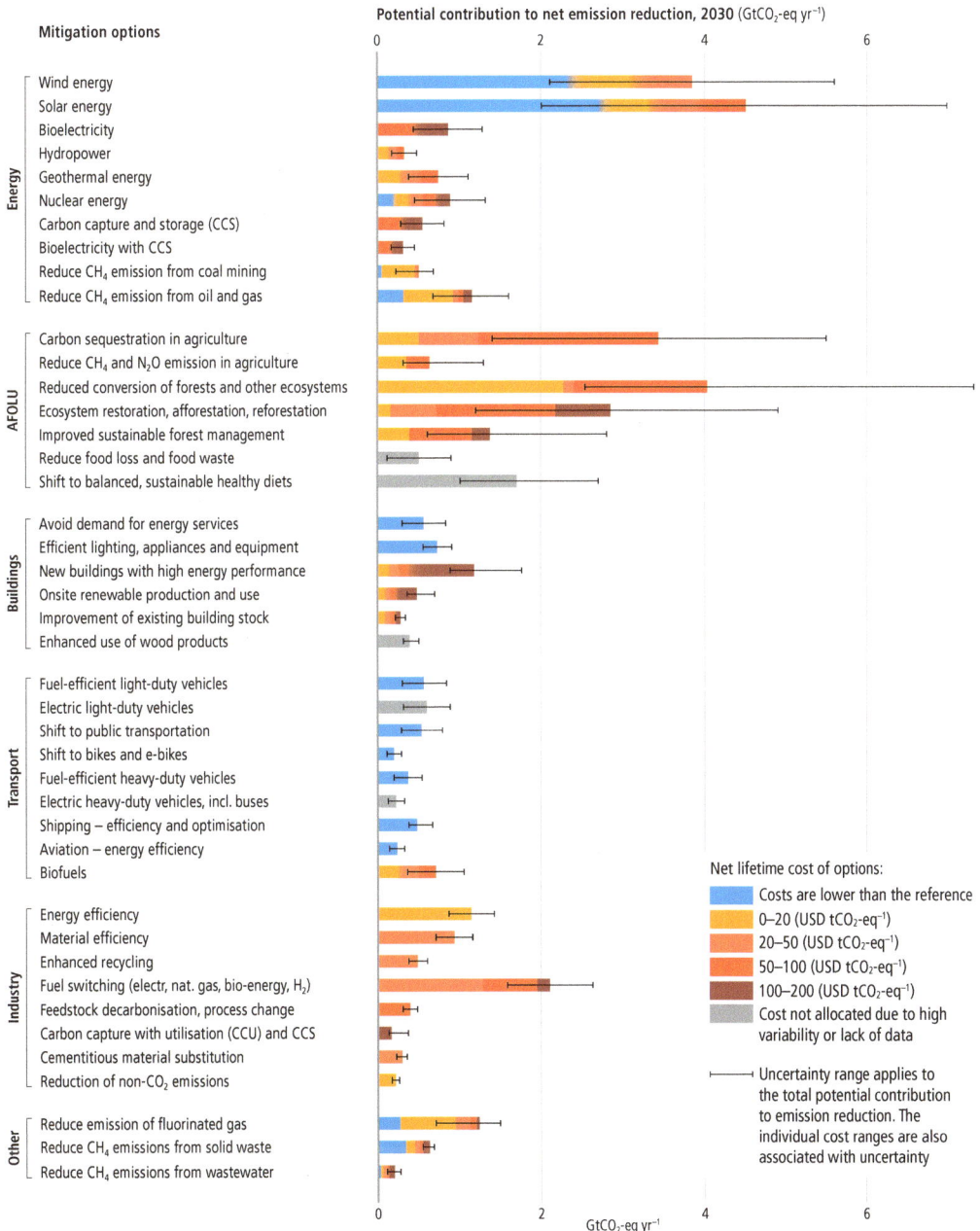

Figure SPM.7 | Overview of mitigation options and their estimated ranges of costs and potentials in 2030.

(continued)

FIGURE 2.2   Overview of mitigation options and their estimated ranges of costs and potentials in 2030 (IPCC Sixth Assessment Report, figure SPM.7) *(Continued)*

Figure SPM.7 (continued): Overview of mitigation options and their estimated ranges of costs and potentials in 2030. Costs shown are net lifetime costs of avoided greenhouse gas emissions. Costs are calculated relative to a reference technology. The assessments per sector were carried out using a common methodology, including definition of potentials, target year, reference scenarios, and cost definitions. The mitigation potential (shown in the horizontal axis) is the quantity of net GHG emission reductions that can be achieved by a given mitigation option relative to a specified emission baseline. Net GHG emission reductions are the sum of reduced emissions and/or enhanced sinks. The baseline used consists of current policy (around 2019) reference scenarios from the AR6 scenarios database (25/75 percentile values). The assessment relies on approximately 175 underlying sources, that together give a fair representation of emission reduction potentials across all regions. The mitigation potentials are assessed independently for each option and are not necessarily additive. {12.2.1, 12.2.2} The length of the solid bars represents the mitigation potential of an option. The error bars display the full ranges of the estimates for the total mitigation potentials. Sources of uncertainty for the cost estimates include assumptions on the rate of technological advancement, regional differences, and economies of scale, among others. Those uncertainties are not displayed in the figure. Potentials are broken down into cost categories, indicated by different colours (see legend). Only discounted lifetime monetary costs are considered. Where a gradual colour transition is shown, the breakdown of the potential into cost categories is not well known or depends heavily on factors such as geographical location, resource availability, and regional circumstances, and the colours indicate the range of estimates. Costs were taken directly from the underlying studies (mostly in the period 2015–2020) or recent datasets. No correction for inflation was applied, given the wide cost ranges used. The cost of the reference technologies were also taken from the underlying studies and recent datasets. Cost reductions through technological learning are taken into account.[a]

- When interpreting this figure, the following should be taken into account:
- The mitigation potential is uncertain, as it will depend on the reference technology (and emissions) being displaced, the rate of new technology adoption, and several other factors.
- Cost and mitigation potential estimates were extrapolated from available sectoral studies. Actual costs and potentials would vary by place, context and time.
- Beyond 2030, the relative importance of the assessed mitigation options is expected to change, in particular while pursuing long-term mitigation goals, recognising also that the emphasis for particular options will vary across regions (for specific mitigation options see SPM Sections C4.1, C5.2, C7.3, C8.3 and C9.1).
- Different options have different feasibilities beyond the cost aspects, which are not reflected in the figure (compare with SPM Section E.1).
- The potentials in the cost range USD100–200 tCO$_2$-eq^{-1} may be underestimated for some options.
- Costs for accommodating the integration of variable renewable energy sources in electricity systems are expected to be modest until 2030, and are not included because of complexities in attributing such costs to individual technology options.
- Cost range categories are ordered from low to high. This order does not imply any sequence of implementation.
- Externalities are not taken into account. {12.2, Table 12.3, 6.4, Table 7.3, Supplementary Material Table 9.SM.2, Supplementary Material Table 9.SM.3, 10.6, 11.4, Figure 11.13, Supplementary Material 12.SM.1.2.3}

[a]For nuclear energy, modelled costs for long-term storage of radioactive waste are included.

Source: Figure SPM.7 in IPCC, 2022: Summary for Policymakers (P. R. Shukla, J. Skea, A. Reisinger, R. Slade, R. Fradera, M. Pathak, A. Al Khourdajie, M. Belkacemi, R. van Diemen, A. Hasija, G. Lisboa, S. Luz, J. Malley, D. McCollum, S. Some, P. Vyas, [eds.]). In: *Climate Change 2022: Mitigation of Climate Change. Contribution of Working Group III to the Sixth Assessment Report of the Intergovernmental Panel on Climate Change* (P. R. Shukla, J. Skea, R. Slade, A. Al Khourdajie, R. van Diemen, D. McCollum, M. Pathak, S. Some, P. Vyas, R. Fradera, M. Belkacemi, A. Hasija, G. Lisboa, S. Luz, J. Malley, [eds.]). Cambridge University Press, Cambridge, UK and New York, NY, USA. doi: 10.1017/9781009157926.001. Reproduced with permission from IPCC. Further permission required for reuse.
Note: CCS = carbon capture and sequestration; CH$_4$ = methane; CO$_2$ =carbon dioxide; GtCO$_2$e^{-1} = gigatonnes carbon dioxide equivalent; H$_2$ = hydrogen; N$_2$O = nitrous oxide.

The effect of deployment today on future cost of technologies

What matters for climate change is the total amount of carbon emitted over the long term. It is therefore critical to consider the impact of investments in technologies today on the future cost of emissions reductions (Gillingham and Stock 2018). If current adoption has positive spillover effects on future costs, then a static cost-benefit analysis will be biased against switching to green technologies.

Current adoption of technologies can improve their future viability.

Dynamic costs can differ from static costs because of factors that firms may not fully internalize (Gillingham and Stock 2018). Adoption of current technology can reduce future costs in the presence of externalities, such as industry-level learning-by-doing, research and development (R&D) spillovers, and network effects. Technologies that require large and irreversible capital expenditures can lead to lock-in effects and stranded assets if firms are unable to or constrained from optimizing dynamically.

Learning curves

Learning curves for green technologies, which show how production costs drop with cumulative production, demonstrate the dynamic cost considerations. A positive learning rate—defined as the decrease in cost or price observed upon a doubling of cumulative market size—has been observed in many green technologies, including solar photovoltaic (PV), wind, and battery storage.

Way et al. (2022) document the long-run cost trajectories and total deployment of major energy technologies (refer to figure 2.3). On average, the cost of solar, wind, and batteries dropped exponentially, at a rate of almost 10 percent a year since they were first marketed, and deployment increased at about the same pace. In contrast, fossil fuel technologies, such as coal, oil, and gas, saw almost no decline in cost since 1880.

> **The cost of solar, wind, and batteries dropped exponentially with increased production, while the cost of fossil fuels did not.**

FIGURE 2.3   Trends in cost and production of useful energy, 1880–2020

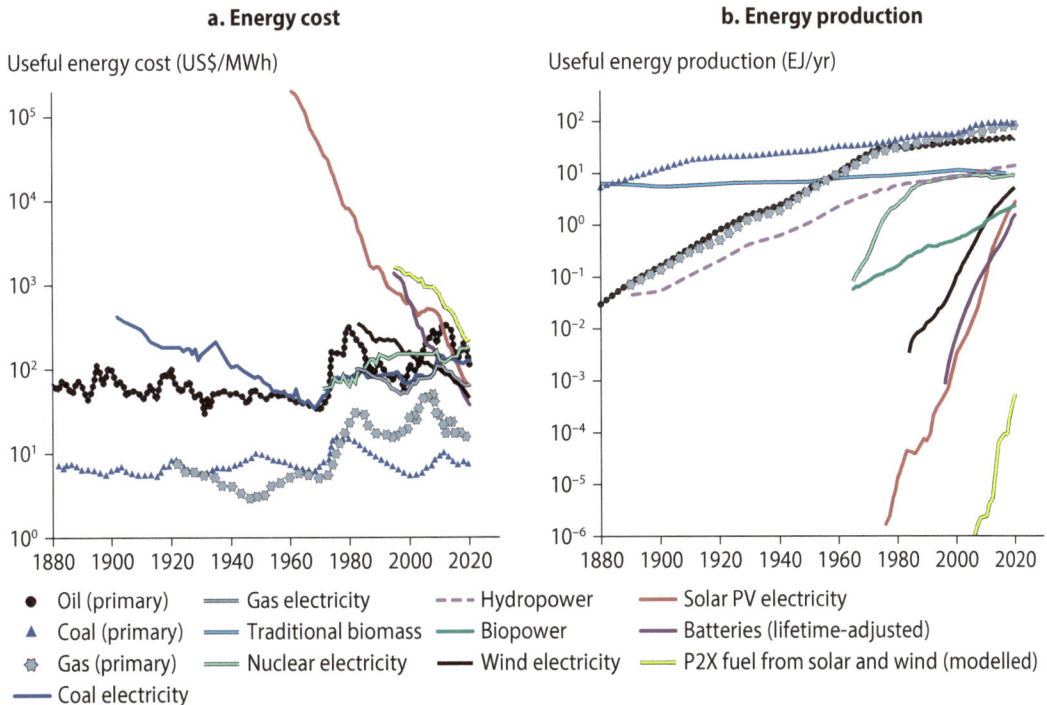

Source: Way et al. 2022. Adapted with permission.
Note: Data for panel a are inflation adjusted. EJ/yr = exajoules per year; MWh = megawatt-hour; P2X = power to X; PV = photovoltaic.

Learning curves matter because if deployment has a causal impact on future costs, a faster transition can be cheaper. Way et al. (2022) show that accounting for learning curves predicts solar PV, wind, and battery deployment better than conventional forecasts, which overestimate costs and underestimate deployment rates. They estimate that accounting for learning, a faster green energy transition results in large overall net savings even without accounting for averted climate damage or co-benefits of climate policy.

Externalities such as R&D spillovers strengthen the rationale for government interventions to encourage adoption in the early phase of the transition. Gerarden (2023) presents evidence of such R&D spillovers in Germany, where a consumer subsidy for solar power caused international firms to innovate more, leading to lower prices and increased adoption elsewhere. He estimates that 86 percent of the benefits of the lower cost came from innovation that occurred outside Germany, suggesting large spillover benefits. (Refer to special focus 2.1, at the end of this chapter.)

An optimistic view: Technological tipping points and breakthroughs

It has been argued that thanks in part to these learning effects, tipping points are likely to be met by 2030 for crucial low-carbon solutions in sectors representing 90 percent of emissions, making them competitive in key markets (Systemiq 2021; refer to figure 2.4). Important tipping points have already occurred: The LCOE of solar and wind fell below that of new coal and gas in 2018, leading solar and wind to account for more than 75 percent of total new capacity additions globally in 2022 (Systemiq 2023). Unsubsidized battery electric vehicles (BEVs) are expected to reach purchase price parity with internal combustion engine (ICE) vehicles by 2025–26 in major regions (BloombergNEF 2023). Green ammonia is projected to be economically viable within the next decade, with implications for fertilizers and sea transport. Green hydrogen is also taking off, with major projects expanding rapidly around the world (Systemiq 2023). Attainment of these tipping points is presented as an opportunity for governments and the private sector to step up investment, policies, and collaboration. But the benefit for any single player is likely to require coordinated action by all major players.

Differences in expectations about the strength of learning curves can lead to different investment paths and feedback loops. For example, if many economic agents expect large declines in costs because of learning, the resulting investments and increased scale of production will generate significant cost reductions. In contrast, if agents have more conservative expectations, their reluctance to invest will imply lower learning and cost savings. Multiple dynamic equilibria may thus exist, some based on optimistic self-fulfilling expectations leading to early viability of green technologies and others based on less optimistic paths.[2] The goal in this report is not to assess the plausibility of these alternative visions but to identify the types of policy actions needed under different scenarios.

Different technologies have different "tipping points."

FIGURE 2.4   Tipping points by sector: Historical progress and indicative future timeline

Low carbon solution maturity

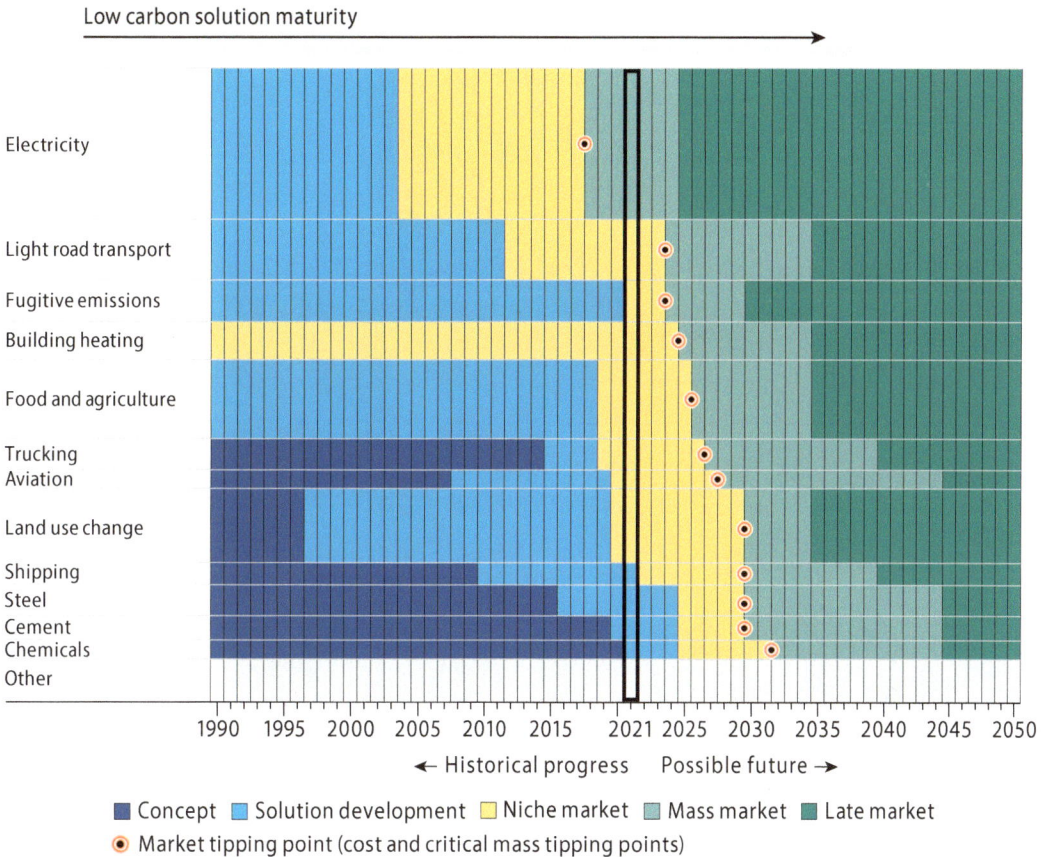

← Historical progress   Possible future →

■ Concept ■ Solution development ☐ Niche market ■ Mass market ■ Late market
⦿ Market tipping point (cost and critical mass tipping points)

Source: Systemiq 2021, © Systemiq. Adapted with permission from Systemiq; further permission required for reuse.
Note: Sectors are sized according to 2019–20 emissions impact. Tipping points exist when a set of conditions are reached that allow new technologies or practices to outcompete incumbents. After a tipping point is crossed, reinforcing feedback loops take hold that drive self-reinforcing progress, so that greater deployment of the solution encourages even faster deployment.

Recent research suggests that the pace of learning may differ significantly across industries. Learning rates are estimated to be lower for less standardized and more complex technologies (Malhotra and Schmidt 2020). Complex technologies face barriers to both learning-by-doing and interproject spillovers because of the high cost of experimentation, long development cycles, and the high cost of coordination in large value chains. Customizing technologies hinders scalability and the development of standardized, replicable knowledge, further slowing technological progress (as in the case of nuclear and bioenergy with carbon capture and storage technologies). Expectations of the evolution of other green technologies cannot therefore be based solely on the dramatic learning seen previously in technologies such as standardized solar PV modules.

The pace of learning differs with inherent technology characteristics.

Lessons from the development of solar PV

The history of how the price of solar power fell illustrates the role of innovation and production subsidies in improving technology viability and consumer subsidies in boosting demand and further reducing costs.

The United States' technology push

In response to the 1970s oil crisis, the United States pioneered innovations in the solar industry through a government-funded technology push strategy. Between 1974 and 1981, the federal government invested US$1.7 billion in photovoltaic (PV) research and development (R&D), creating institutions like the Department of Energy and the Solar Energy Research Institute (now the National Renewable Energy Laboratory). Government support funded demonstration projects, laboratory testing, R&D subsidies, homeowner tax credits, and a commercialization program. Federal R&D spending was more than double private investments. Although it lost its global PV leadership in the mid-1980s, the United States contributed to significant technological improvements: Cell efficiencies tripled, costs fell by a factor of five, and reliability sharply increased, with the failure rate of solar modules dropping from 45 percent to 0.1 percent.

Japan's niche markets

In the 1980s, as US PV firms were exiting the industry, Japanese conglomerates entered the market, initially focusing on niche applications in satellites and consumer electronics. In 1994, after these markets became saturated, the Japanese government launched a residential solar subsidy program that contributed to a 22-fold growth in the Japanese PV industry by 2003. In addition to providing demand subsidies, Japan's Ministry of International Trade and Industry actively promoted knowledge spillovers among large conglomerates like Sharp and Kyocera. R&D focused on niche markets, particularly thin-film silicon, allowed for efficiency improvements and integration into consumer electronics. Although these markets were ultimately insufficient for firms to achieve economies of scale, Japan played a crucial role in advancing PV technology and demonstrating the benefits of scaling up.

Germany's demand-pull policy

Germany's Renewable Energy Law (EEG), passed in 2000, transformed the global PV market by creating a far bigger market opportunity than existed before. The EEG established feed-in tariffs (FiTs), which guaranteed substantial revenues for electricity from renewable sources, such as solar, causing a boom in demand for solar modules and cells. This policy created opportunities to realize economies of scale, enabling equipment providers to design machines specifically for PV applications. The EEG attracted significant investment, allowing PV start-ups to scale up production. Between 2004 and 2010, Germany produced half of the world's new solar installations. By 2012, PV module prices had dropped to 16 percent of their pre-EEG level, with the technological frontier shifting from cell design to equipment design.[a] Germany's demand-pull policy led to increased innovation by international firms, resulting in lower prices and increased adoption elsewhere (Gerarden 2023).

China's scale-up

China's contribution to the development of low-cost PV was initially facilitated by demand from Germany and a combination of internal factors, including entrepreneurial activity, municipal government support, and the use of expertise from other sectors, such as semiconductors and high-volume manufacturing. The rise in demand for PV, triggered by the German FiT, encouraged Chinese firms to rapidly scale up to meet the growing market. China also implemented a series of local production and R&D subsidies starting in 2006 and intensified demand support in 2010 (Banares-Sanchez et al. 2024) after external demand fell following the global financial crisis and the phase-out of Germany's FiT. Between 2004 and 2020, the number of solar firms in China increased more than sixfold to 1,500 (Banares-Sanchez et al. 2024). These firms not only increased production, they also innovated in products and processes (an estimated 25 percent of their patents were related to efficiency improvements). As competition and innovations intensified, costs continued to fall. The average global price of solar panels fell 75 percent between 2010 and 2015, with Chinese firms leading the expansion of production, producing two-thirds of the world's solar panels during this period (Gerarden 2023).

Policy insights

The trajectory of the solar industry offers valuable policy insights. Banares-Sanchez et al. (2024) find substantial benefits to China from its solar policy, which yielded benefits that exceeded costs by a factor of four (ignoring climate change externalities). The existence of cross-country spillovers and learning suggests that subsidies have an amplified impact on the adoption of similar technologies. This finding underscores the importance of international coordination in accelerating the development of technologies needed to address climate change.

Note: Except where otherwise indicated, this special focus is based on Nemet (2019).
a. A notable innovation is the invention of "turnkey" solar manufacturing equipment, which enabled firms without deep expertise in solar technology to quickly jump into PV module and cell manufacturing (refer to Chan 2024).

Notes

1. The LCOE is defined as the energy price (in dollars per unit of energy produced) for which the net present value of investment is zero.
2. This idea builds on Arrow's (1962) early insights about how experience can lower costs as well as later applications of how, under network effects and dynamic spillovers, different beliefs can yield different investment paths and random events can either lock the path of technologies to inferior ones or push the economy toward a different equilibrium (Arthur 1989; David 1985).

References

Arrow, K. J. 1962. "The Economic Implications of Learning by Doing." *Review of Economic Studies* 29 (3): 155–73.

Arthur, W. B. 1989. "Competing Technologies, Increasing Returns, and Lock-In by Historical Events." *Economic Journal* 99 (394): 116–31.

Banares-Sanchez, I., R. Burgess, D. Laszlo, P. Simpson, J. Van Reenen, and Y. Wang 2024. "Ray of Hope? Chinese Innovation, Green Industrial Policy and the Rise of Solar Energy." Unpublished paper. https://en.cafr.cn/Events/NBER/Ray%20of%20Hope%20China%20 and%20the%20Rise%20of%20Solar%20Energy.pdf.

BloombergNEF. 2023. "Electric Vehicle Outlook 2023." Executive summary. https:// assets.bbhub.io/professional/sites/24/2431510_BNEFElectricVehicleOutlook2023 _ExecSummary.pdf.

Chan, K. 2024. "Chinese Solar and the German Paradox." *High Capacity* (blog), April 20, 2024. https://www.high-capacity.com/p/chinese-solar-and-the-german-paradox.

David, P. A. 1985. "Clio and the Economics of QWERTY." *American Economic Review* 75 (2): 332–37.

Gerarden, T. D. 2023. "Demanding Innovation: The Impact of Consumer Subsidies on Solar Panel Production Costs." *Management Science* 69 (12): 7799–820. https://doi.org/10.1287 /mnsc.2022.4662.

Gillingham, K., and J. H. Stock. 2018. "The Cost of Reducing Greenhouse Gas Emissions." *Journal of Economic Perspectives* 32 (4): 53–72. https://doi.org/10.1257/jep.32.4.53.

IEA (International Energy Agency). 2024. *Global EV Outlook 2024: Moving towards Increased Affordability*. Paris: IEA. https://www.iea.org/reports/global-ev-outlook-2024.

IPCC (Intergovernmental Panel on Climate Change). 2023. *Climate Change 2022: Mitigation of Climate Change*. Working Group III contribution to the Sixth Assessment Report of the Intergovernmental Panel on Climate Change. Cambridge, UK: Cambridge University Press.

IRENA (International Renewable Energy Agency). 2023. *Renewable Power Generation Costs in 2022*. Abu Dhabi, United Arab Emirates: IRENA. https://www.irena.org /Publications/2023/Aug/Renewable-Power-Generation-Costs-in-2022.

Malhotra, A., and T. S. Schmidt. 2020. "Accelerating Low-Carbon Innovation." *Joule* 4 (11): 2259–67. https://doi.org/10.1016/j.joule.2020.09.004.

Nemet, G. F. 2019. *How Solar Energy Became Cheap: A Model for Low-Carbon Innovation.* New York: Routledge.

Systemiq. 2021. *The Paris Effect—COP26 Edition: How Tipping Points Can Accelerate and Deliver a Net Zero Economy.* London: Systemiq. https://www.systemiq.earth/the -paris-effect-cop26-edition/.

Systemiq. 2023. *The Breakthrough Effect: How to Trigger a Cascade of Tipping Points to Accelerate the Net Zero Transition.* London: Systemiq. https://www.systemiq.earth/wp -content/uploads/2023/01/The-Breakthrough-Effect.pdf.

Way, R., M. C. Ives, P. Mealy, and J. D. Farmer. 2022. "Empirically Grounded Technology Forecasts and the Energy Transition." *Joule* 6 (9): 2057–82. https://doi.org/10.1016/j .joule.2022.08.009.

How is East Asia and Pacific contributing to the development and global diffusion of green technologies?

3

China and East Asia Pacific's diverse contributions

East Asia and Pacific (EAP) is contributing to the emergence and adoption of green technologies through innovation, investment, and trade. China has emerged as a leader in green innovation, thanks to significant support for research and development (R&D) from the state. Its large investments are bringing forward the viability of green technologies by realizing economies of scale and accelerating movements down learning curves in areas like renewable energy and battery storage. The more granular division of labor and high levels of competition across countries in the region, such as Viet Nam in solar panels and Thailand in vehicle components, have led to significant reductions in the costs of many products. As a global manufacturing hub, EAP is also uniquely positioned to harness the green transition to boost its own economic growth.

The growing role of China in developing new green technologies

Tracking the development of green technologies across countries is difficult, because production technologies that are invented but not patented cannot be observed. However, patents can serve as a result-based proxy of technological progress, as they reflect the direction of R&D within industries. This section draws on data from the World Intellectual Property Organization and the Worldwide Patent Statistical Database to

- Identify the countries that have applied for patents in particular technologies and
- Document the extent to which the innovation process has been integrated into global innovation networks.

EAP is playing an increasing role in technology development. Patent output for green technologies increased in EAP between 1995 and 2020 (refer to figure 3.1).[1]

China has increasingly contributed to the development of new green technologies.

FIGURE 3.1   EAP contributions to green patenting, 1995–2020

a. Number of green patent applications

Green patent applications (thousands)

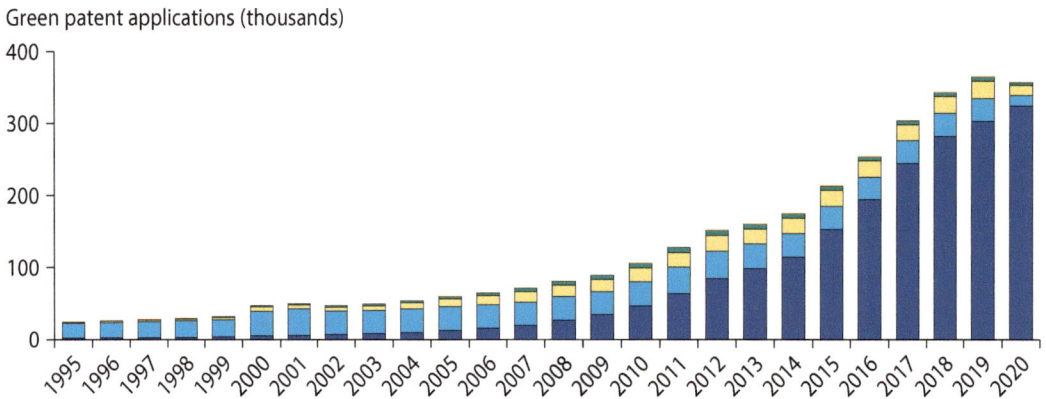

b. Share of global total

Green patent applications (% of global total)

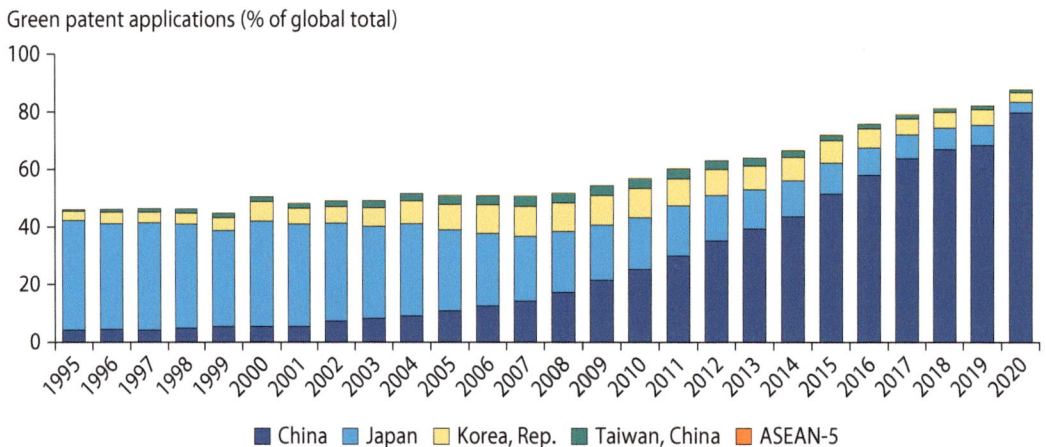

■ China   ■ Japan   ■ Korea, Rep.   ■ Taiwan, China   ■ ASEAN-5

Source: Data from the World Intellectual Property Organization (WIPO) (https://www.wipo.int/en/web/patentscope).
Note: Patents are identified as *green* based on the International Patent Classification green inventory of the WIPO. Green patents relate to one of four areas: (1) alternative energy production, such as biofuels and renewables; (2) transportation, including hybrid and electric vehicles, rail vehicles, and marine vessels; (3) energy conservation, including batteries and measurement of electric consumption; and (4) nuclear power generation. ASEAN-5 = Indonesia, Malaysia, the Philippines, Singapore, and Thailand; EAP = East Asia and Pacific.

Initially, Japan—and to a lesser extent the Republic of Korea—contributed most to this rise. Since the early 2000s, China has steadily increased its patenting output.[2] Green innovation capacity has remained almost negligible in developing EAP outside China.

Innovations in renewable energy used to account for the bulk of green patents (refer to figure 3.2). In the 1990s and early 2000s, Germany led the world in solar patents. Since the 2010s, East Asia has boosted its footprint, with Korean companies Samsung and LG and Japanese companies Panasonic, Hitachi, and Toshiba filing hundreds of patents in solar energy (IEA 2021).

> **Renewables and related technologies account for the bulk of new green-tech developments.**

FIGURE 3.2 **Patent applications for green technology, China and rest of world, 2000–20**

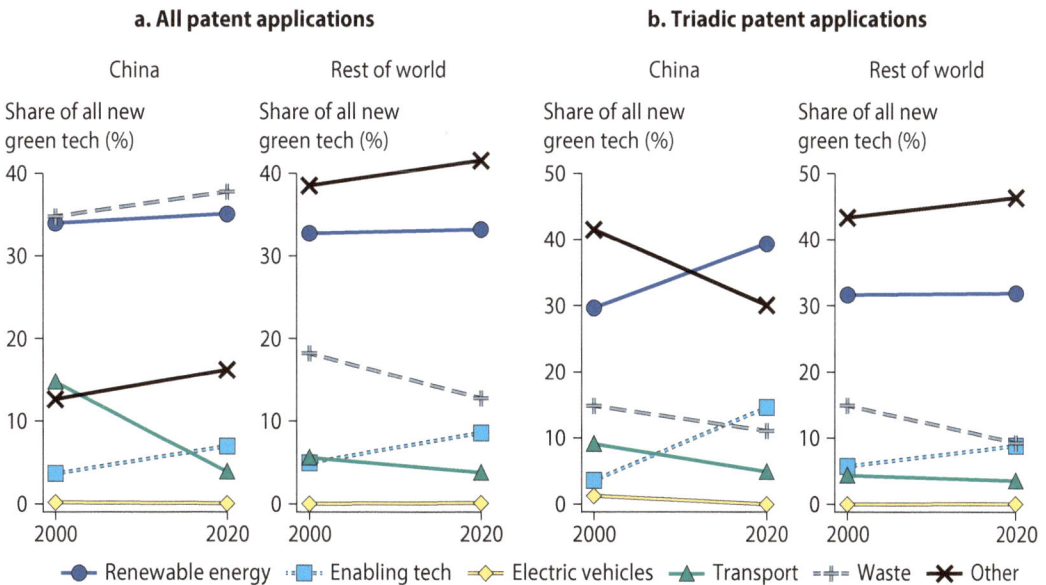

a. All patent applications

b. Triadic patent applications

Source: Data from the World Intellectual Property Organization (https://www.wipo.int/en/web/patentscope).
Note: Enabling refers to technologies that enable the use of renewable energy, such as energy storage devices and smart grids.
Triadic patents are patents applied for with the European, US, and world patent offices.

The invention market was shaken up as renewable technologies matured: The entry of new inventors declined in most countries except China. Chinese applicants increased their innovation efforts and became leaders in patents for silicon production, ingots, wafers, and modules (Carvalho, Dechezleprêtre, and Glachant 2017). The overall pace of patenting in renewable energy technologies slowed, peaking around 2010 and declining thereafter. Since then, the focus has shifted toward enabling technologies—technologies that enable the deployment and facilitate the integration of renewable energy sources, such as batteries, smart grids, and hydrogen. The increase in battery patenting is driven by the rapid development and industrialization of lithium-ion battery technology for electric mobility. Japan and Korea have filed a large number of patents related to batteries and electric vehicles (EVs). Samsung, Panasonic, and LG accounted for almost a fifth of all battery patent applications between 2000 and 2019. Between 2000 and 2019, Toyota was the top inventor of low-carbon technologies worldwide, and most of its patenting output related to EVs (IEA 2021). Chinese companies such as Contemporary Amperex Technology Co., Limited (CATL), the world's largest EV battery maker, and BYD, the world's largest producer of EVs, significantly increased their share of patents after 2017.

China's patent quality has improved, but it remains relatively low, including for green patents. Thanks partly to public support, patenting capacity in China has steadily increased since the early 2000s. Patent quality, however, still pales relative to that of other advanced economies. The number of triadic patents—patents filed in the European, US, and world patent offices—can be considered a proxy for quality, as firms likely incur the extra cost of filing in a patent office outside their borders only for patents they consider sufficiently valuable (Dechezleprêtre, Ménière, and Mohnen 2017). In contrast with the significant increase in domestic patenting capacity, the number of triadic patents filed by Chinese inventors rose more slowly between 1995 and 2020 (refer to figure 3.3, panel a). Compared with the global share of all green patents (refer to figure 3.1, panel b), the global share of Chinese triadic patents remains relatively low (refer to figure 3.3, panel b). China performs better when patent quality is measured based on the number of times a patent is cited by other patents (Green and Stapleton 2025) (refer to figure 3.4).

China's patents remain of variable quality, with few triadic patents.

FIGURE 3.3   EAP's contribution to green triadic patents, 1995–2020

a. Number of triadic green patent applications

Number of applications (thousands)

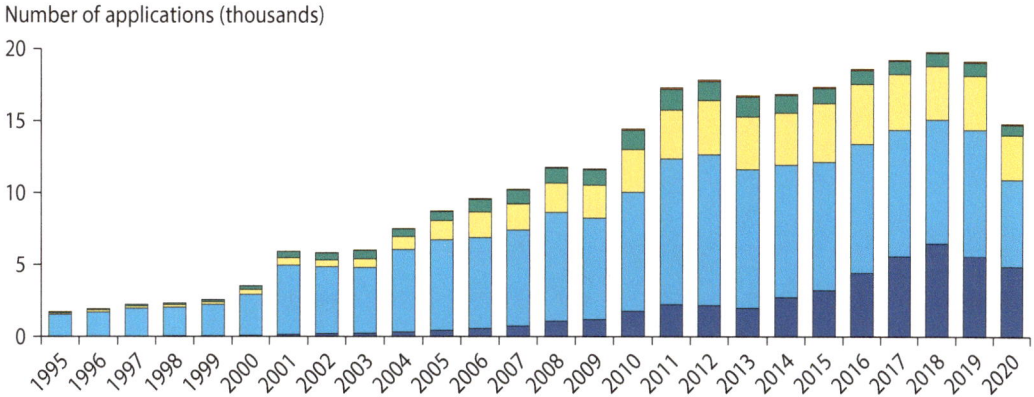

b. Global share of triadic green patents

Percent

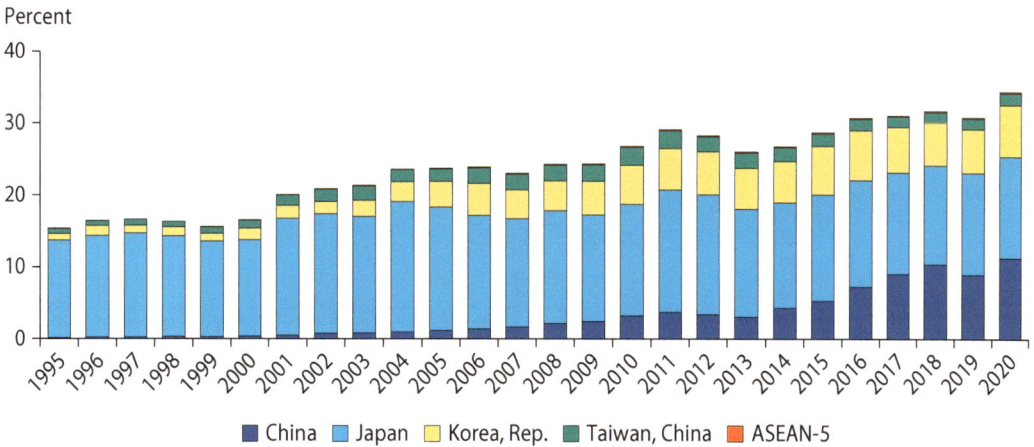

■ China ■ Japan ☐ Korea, Rep. ■ Taiwan, China ■ ASEAN-5

Source: Data from the World Intellectual Property Organization (https://www.wipo.int/en/web/patentscope).
Note: Triadic patents are patents applied for with the European, US, and world patent offices. ASEAN-5 = Indonesia, Malaysia, the Philippines, Singapore, and Thailand.

Chinese inventions tend to be produced domestically, without collaboration with international inventors (refer to figure 3.5). The share of international co-inventions is much larger in the United States (IEA 2022c). Corrocher, Grabner, and Morrison (2024) argue that green technologies are characterized by substantial complexity and uncertainty and, thus, green co-inventions hinge on local absorptive capacity and the ability to attract complementary capabilities of leading green innovators.

China's patent quality improves when measured by the number of citations received.

FIGURE 3.4   **Alternative quality-adjusted measures of China's green patents**

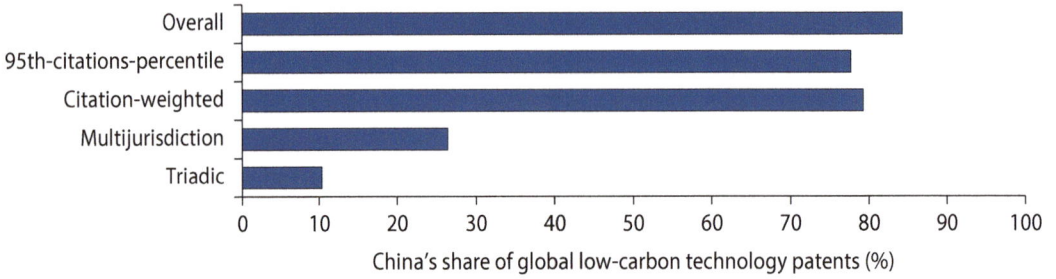

Source: Green and Stapleton 2025.

Note: 95th-citations-percentile = counting patents at 95th percentile of citations; citation-weighted = patent count weighted by citations; multijurisdiction = counting patents filed in multiple countries or legal jurisdictions; overall = all patents; triadic = counting patents filed in the European, Japan, and US patent offices.

Most Chinese patents for climate change mitigation technologies do not involve international co-inventors.

FIGURE 3.5   **Co-invention in green patents across countries**

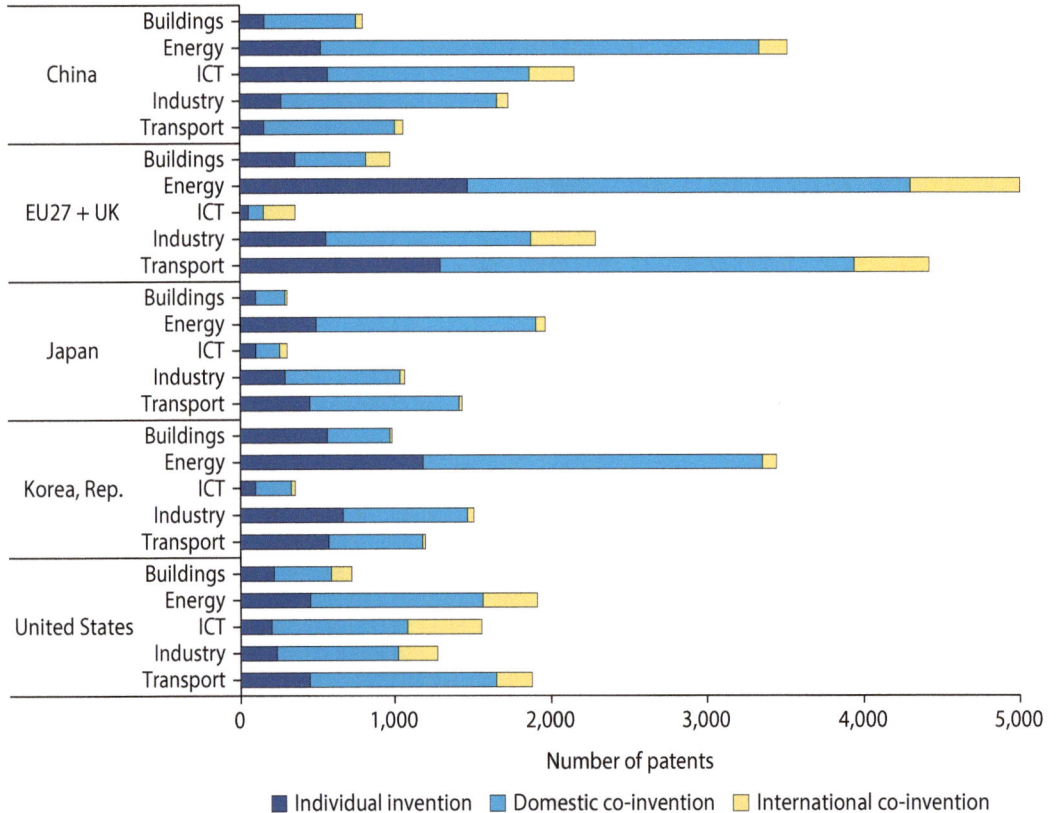

Source: Data from the Organisation for Economic Co-operation and Development (http://oe.cd/ipstats).

Note: EU27 + UK = 27 countries in the European Union plus the United Kingdom; ICT = information and communication technology.

The dearth of international collaboration may partly reflect concerns about China's ability to protect intellectual property rights (IPRs) adequately. The lengthy litigation between Chinese company Sinovel and the US company American Superconductor over technology to enhance energy efficiency in wind turbines, which involved multiple lawsuits and costly jurisdiction shopping, demonstrates that protecting green IPRs is complicated and costly (Yang and Chen 2017).

Failure to respect IPRs can have a lasting negative effect on innovation, reducing the quantity, value, and impact of patents (Curti et al. 2023). These adverse repercussions are attributed not to resource diversion (as targeted firms do not reduce R&D) but to the leakage of proprietary information. The effects can spread to the business partners of affected firms, further dampening innovation output. Box 3.1 discusses the opposing effects of IPRs on the development and diffusion of green technology.

Box 3.1. Do intellectual property rights encourage discovery without impeding the diffusion of green technologies?

Intellectual property rights (IPRs) can be contentious. By ensuring that inventors benefit from their inventions, they can spur technology transfer. They can also impede such transfer, however, because monopoly rights associated with IPRs grant significant market power to innovators.

The role of IPRs may be heightened with the increase in the absorptive capacity of the recipient country. Countries with less information on available technologies and poorer access to skilled workers may benefit less from weak IPR regimes, as even without such protection they would not be able to replicate or imitate the technology (Maskus and Penubarti 1995).

Dussaux, Dechezleprêtre, and Glachant (2022) explore the relationship between the stringency of IPR regimes and cross-border flows of climate change mitigation technologies. In both Organisation for Economic Co-operation and Development (OECD) and non-OECD countries, stricter IPR regimes tend not to impede the transfer of climate change mitigation technology. However, some significant effects are reported. Stronger IPR regimes are associated with higher foreign direct investment in solar photovoltaic (PV), wind power, and cleaner vehicles. The relationship with imports of capital goods is less robust: The association with stricter IPRs is positive in the case of hydro and cleaner vehicles and negative in the case of solar PV and thermal equipment. This negative association may reflect the fact that non-OECD countries may become less dependent on imports and foster more

(continued)

Box 3.1.   Do intellectual property rights encourage discovery without impeding the diffusion of green technologies? *(Continued)*

innovation domestically. It is also possible that technology diffuses through other channels, such as international joint ventures, which are common in China.

The role of IPRs may be overstated by focusing on intellectual property (IP) law (de jure IPRs) rather than IP enforcement (de facto IPR) because of political economy and governance capability considerations. Athreye et al. (2023) consider a longer period of analysis than Dussaux, Dechezleprêtre, and Glachant (2022)—originally 1997–2007 then extended to 2018—and differentiate between de jure and de facto IPR regimes. These changes in the estimation framework yield results that are significantly different from those of Dussaux and colleagues. They find that strong de facto IPRs are associated with less transfer of climate change mitigation technologies. They argue that governments can rely on several measures to lower the barriers posed by IPRs and promote technology transfers, including the regulation of voluntary licenses, exemptions to patentability, exceptions to patent rights, and parallel importation.

Declining international collaboration may dampen the quality of future innovation. Aghion et al. (2023) show that recent US policy restrictions, such as the 2018 China Initiative, reduced China–US research collaboration.[3] It reduced both the volume and quality of Chinese researchers who had collaborated with US researchers compared with those who collaborated with European researchers. But innovation is not a zero-sum game: Such restrictions may hurt not only Chinese innovation but also the innovation of US firms (refer to figure 3.6). Although this evidence is not specific to green technologies, it is reasonable to expect that the restrictions on the flow of ideas can harm the global availability of green innovations.

Contribution of Chinese investments in green technologies to global diffusion

Measured by investment expenditures, China leads the world in green technology deployment. China funded almost two-thirds of the world's growth in total investment in the energy transition between 2023 and 2024 (IEA 2024b). In 2024, its clean energy accounted for one-third of the world's investments in clean energy (refer to figure 3.7); it also invested heavily in other sectors, such as electrified transport (BloombergNEF 2025).

Policy restrictions such as the 2018 "China Initiative" may have hurt not only Chinese but also US innovations.

FIGURE 3.6   Effect of the 2018 China Initiative on patenting output

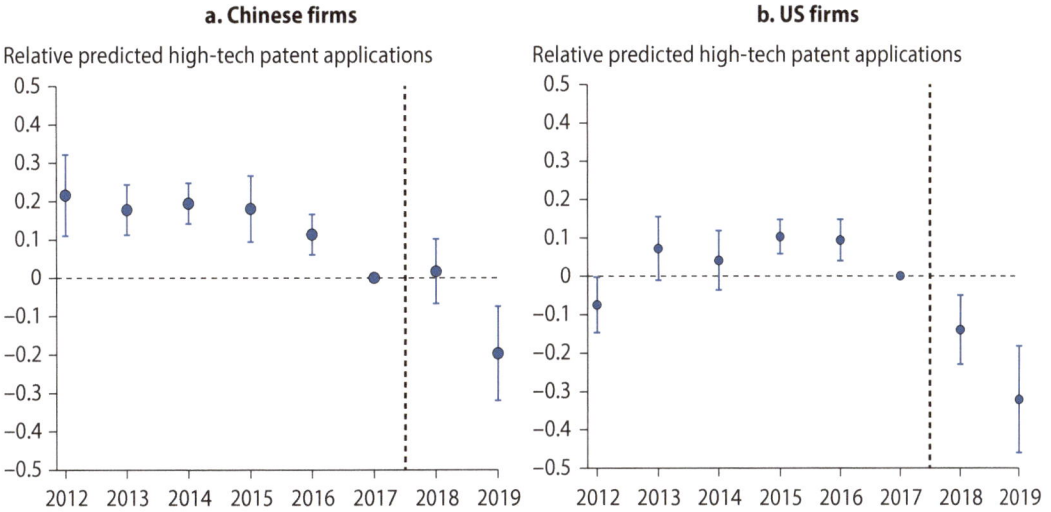

a. Chinese firms

Relative predicted high-tech patent applications

b. US firms

Relative predicted high-tech patent applications

Source: Cao et al. 2024.

Note: Figure shows coefficient estimates with 95 percent confidence interval from an event study on the number of high-tech patent applications worldwide before and after 2018, comparing inventors who had prior collaboration with inventors from China (panel a) and those who collaborated with inventors from the United States (panel b).

In 2024, China accounted for one-third of the world's investments in clean energy.

FIGURE 3.7   Investments in clean energy, 2024

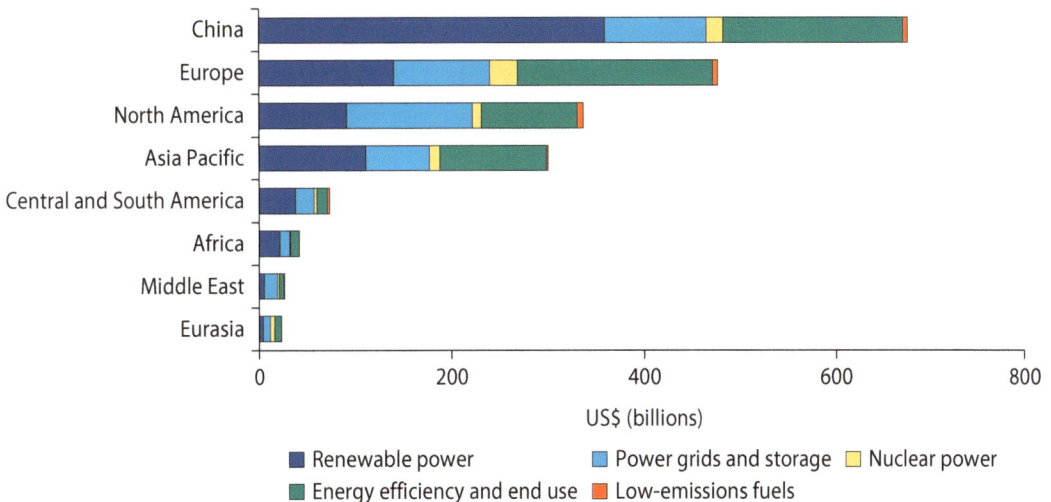

US$ (billions)

■ Renewable power   ■ Power grids and storage   ■ Nuclear power
■ Energy efficiency and end use   ■ Low-emissions fuels

Source: IEA 2024b.

Note: Asia Pacific includes Australia and New Zealand and excludes China.

China was the largest investor in energy transition projects every year over the past decade, thanks to substantial government support. From 2009 until 2020, when other advanced economies started ramping up their own green transition, China's government interventions in green sectors increased at a faster rate than the rest of the world's (refer to figure B3.2.1 in box 3.2). These investments benefited China's own transition and likely create positive spillovers to other countries. Scaling up production may have helped Chinese producers "ride down" learning curves and exploit economies of scale and scope in key technologies. Banares-Sanchez et al. (2024) show how local production subsidies increased process-efficiency innovations among Chinese solar manufacturers. When learning curves are present, as they are in the battery industry, subsidies have a magnified impact on adoption, because of cost reductions and cross-country spillovers.[4] Preliminary evidence from trade data suggests that green products that received government support were eventually exported at lower prices to other emerging economies (refer to box 3.2).

Box 3.2. Are there cross-border spillovers from green subsidies?

As countries adapt to climate change and the green transition, green goods are at the center of trade and industrial policies worldwide. One striking example is the Biden administration's implementation of sweeping tariff hikes in September 2024 on electric vehicles (EVs), batteries, and solar cells from China, including a quadrupling of the tariff on EVs, from 25 percent to 100 percent. These tariff hikes continued the trend from the US–China trade war tariffs imposed by the first Trump administration in 2018, which heavily affected green goods. In 2024, the European Union imposed tariff increases of up to 38 percent on Chinese EVs.

At the same time, countries are scaling up subsidies for green technologies (refer to figure B3.2.1). The EU and US tariff hikes took aim at China's efforts to subsidize their industries, which coincided with China's growing share of exports of green goods and declining reliance on imports of green goods from the rest of the world (refer to figure B3.2.2). New subsidies for green technologies in the rest of the world were also introduced at a fast pace since 2020.

(continued)

Box 3.2. Are there cross-border spillovers from green subsidies? *(Continued)*

FIGURE B3.2.1 **Countries are scaling up subsidies for green technologies**

Number of interventions related to green technology

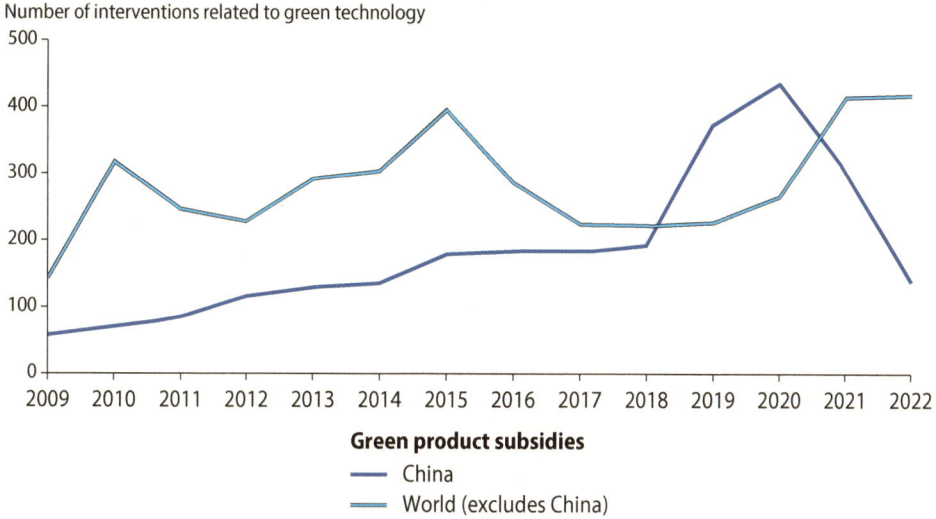

Green product subsidies
— China
— World (excludes China)

Sources: Data from the Global Trade Alert database (https://globaltradealert.org/) on number of interventions; data from Base pour l'Analyse du Commerce International (BACI) (https://www.cepii.fr/CEPII/en/bdd_modele/bdd_modele_item .asp?id=37) on trade flows.

Note: Green goods are goods defined as environmental goods (IMF 2022a), low-carbon technology goods (IMF 2022b), or goods in green value chains (Mealy and Teytelboym 2022; Rosenow and Mealy 2024).

FIGURE B3.2.2 **Green goods account for a growing share of China's exports and a declining share of its total imports**

Green goods trade flow (%)

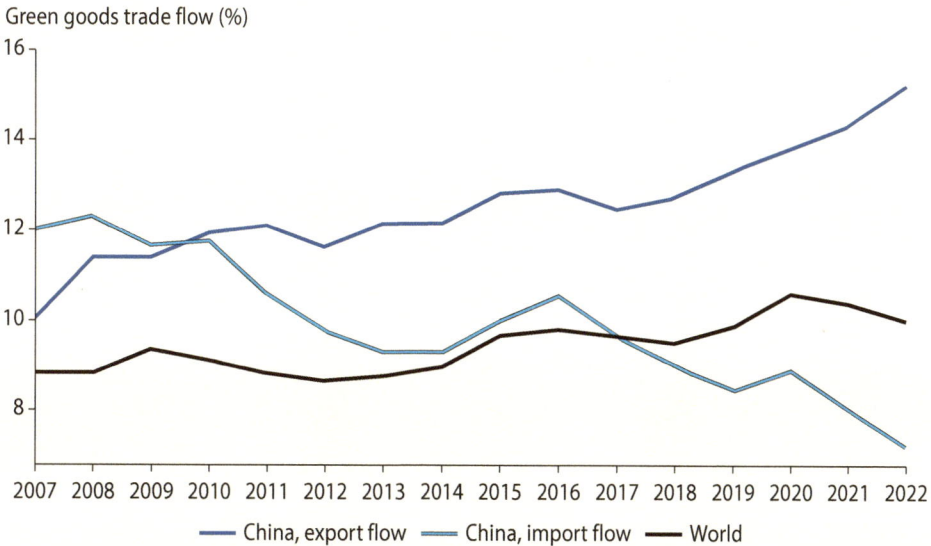

— China, export flow — China, import flow — World

Source: Bilateral trade flow data from Base pour l'Analyse du Commerce International (BACI) (https://www.cepii.fr/CEPII/en /bdd_modele/bdd_modele_item.asp?id=37).

(continued)

Box 3.2.   Are there cross-border spillovers from green subsidies? *(Continued)*

Given the global public good nature of green technologies, understanding the cross-country spillover effects of trade and industrial policies on their production and adoption is crucial. What has been the effect of subsidies from advanced economies and China on other emerging markets? Preliminary evidence based on trade data suggests that global subsidies of green goods have reduced the prices of exports to emerging economies (refer to figure B3.2.3, panel b). A similar trend is observed with green goods that received subsidies in China, although the price differences are not statistically significant because of smaller sample size and fewer variations across goods that received subsidies (refer to figure B3.2.3, panel a).

FIGURE B3.2.3   Green goods receiving government subsidies are eventually exported at lower prices to other emerging economies

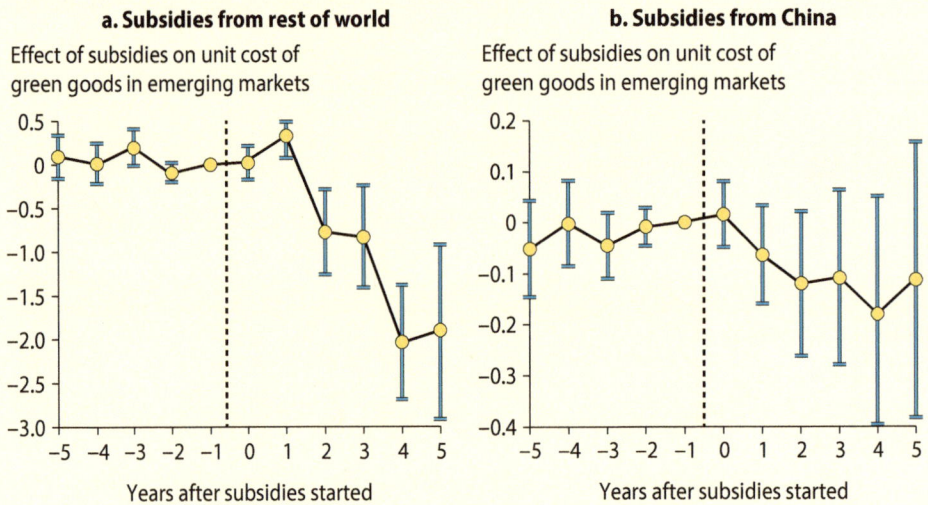

a. Subsidies from rest of world

Effect of subsidies on unit cost of green goods in emerging markets

b. Subsidies from China

Effect of subsidies on unit cost of green goods in emerging markets

Years after subsidies started

Years after subsidies started

Sources: Bilateral trade flow data from Base pour l'Analyse du Commerce International (BACI) (https://www.cepii.fr/CEPII /en/bdd_modele/bdd_modele_item.asp?id=37); 2012–22 data on subsidies from the Global Trade Alert database (https://globaltradealert.org/).

Note: Figure shows difference-in-differences estimates of the impact of subsidies in exporting countries on import prices in emerging market economies. Panel a shows differences in Chinese export prices of green goods receiving subsidies versus not receiving any subsidies. Panel b shows differences in export prices of green goods receiving subsidies from any countries compared with green goods not receiving any subsidies. Prices were calculated as three-year moving averages. Results are conditional on product (HS6) and year fixed effects. Standard errors are clustered at the HS6 product level. HS6 = Harmonized System 6.

Since the late 2000s, the world's green transition has become increasingly reliant on Chinese exports of green goods. The rapid rise in investment in green manufacturing capacity has helped reshape global supply chains, shifting export flows from Europe and the United States to China (refer to figure 3.8). China now dominates the downstream segments of PV manufacturing and EV batteries. Between 2011 and 2022, it invested over US$50 billion in new PV supply capacity. Its share of all manufacturing stages of solar panels exceeded 75 percent in 2021; for key components, such as wafers, its share exceeded 95 percent (IEA 2022a). With substantial backing and subsidies from the Chinese government, CATL was transformed from a business with few employees manufacturing iPod batteries to the world's largest producer of EV batteries (refer to special focus 3.1, at the end of this chapter).[5] The increased geographical concentration of global supply chains has created concerns about their resilience.[6]

China dominates downstream segments of clean energy supply chains.

FIGURE 3.8   **Trade flows of solar PV and EV, by value chain stage, 2016–22**

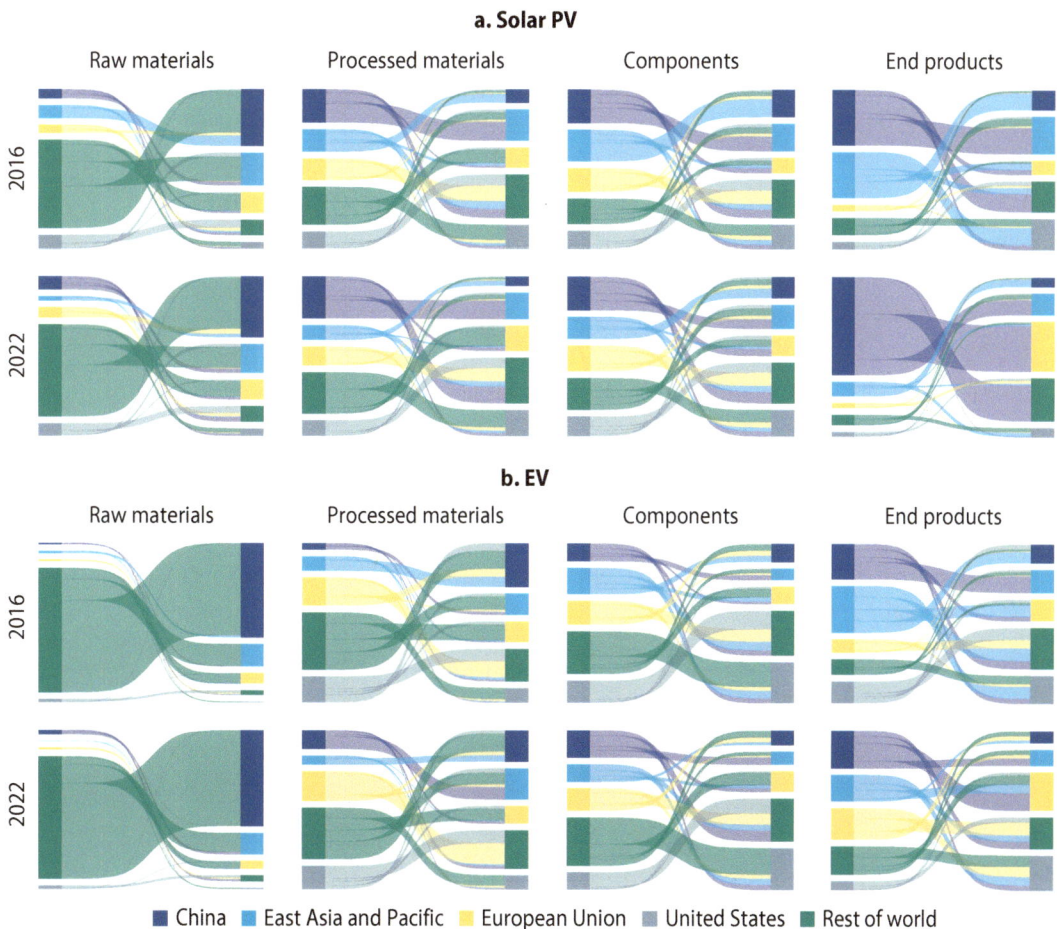

a. Solar PV

b. EV

■ China ■ East Asia and Pacific ■ European Union ■ United States ■ Rest of world

Sources: Bilateral trade data from Base pour l'Analyse du Commerce International (BACI) (https://www.cepii.fr/CEPII/en/bdd_modele /bdd_modele_item.asp?id=37) and classifications in Rosenow and Mealy 2024.
Note: EV = electric vehicle; PV = photovoltaic.

Participation of developing countries in East Asia outside China in green supply chains

As the world, especially the United States, seeks to reduce its dependence on a single country, other countries are increasingly pursuing green industries as a new source of growth. Estimates by the International Energy Agency suggest that clean energy sectors—including clean electricity generation; manufacturing in the solar PV, wind power,

> **Malaysia, Thailand, and Viet Nam have increased their footprints in the solar value chain.**

and battery value chains; and sales of EVs and heat pumps—contributed 10 percent to global GDP growth in 2023 (IEA 2024b). This market is likely to grow as the impacts of global warming become more apparent and demand for climate action intensifies.

Even without considering climate concerns, green industries may offer developing countries several advantages over existing industries. First, some new green industries may have lower barriers to entry, given the lack of established incumbents (for example, refer to the discussion of China's entry into the EV industry in special focus 3.1). Second, green investments may yield higher returns than their dirty counterparts because of greater knowledge spillovers that can be captured domestically (IMF 2024; Martin and Verhoeven 2022).

Some Southeast Asian countries have already leveraged their manufacturing capacity and expertise to increase their footprint in green value chains. Malaysia, Thailand, and Viet Nam have considerable manufacturing capacity in solar PV cells and modules and are cost-competitive (IEA 2022a). In recent years, production has relocated from China to neighboring countries (refer to figure 3.9).[7] The prospects for relocating production in the rest of East Asia are uncertain, in the face of competing countries' industrial policy measures, such as the United States' Inflation Reduction Act (IRA). The IRA's investment tax credits for battery components and wind and solar equipment include provisions to reshore production to the United States, potentially diverting future investment away from the EAP region. Ongoing revisions to these provisions under the new administration add another layer of uncertainty.

> Developing East Asia accounts for a growing share of the solar value chain.

FIGURE 3.9   **Share of solar value chain imports, China and other economies, 2013–22**

Percent

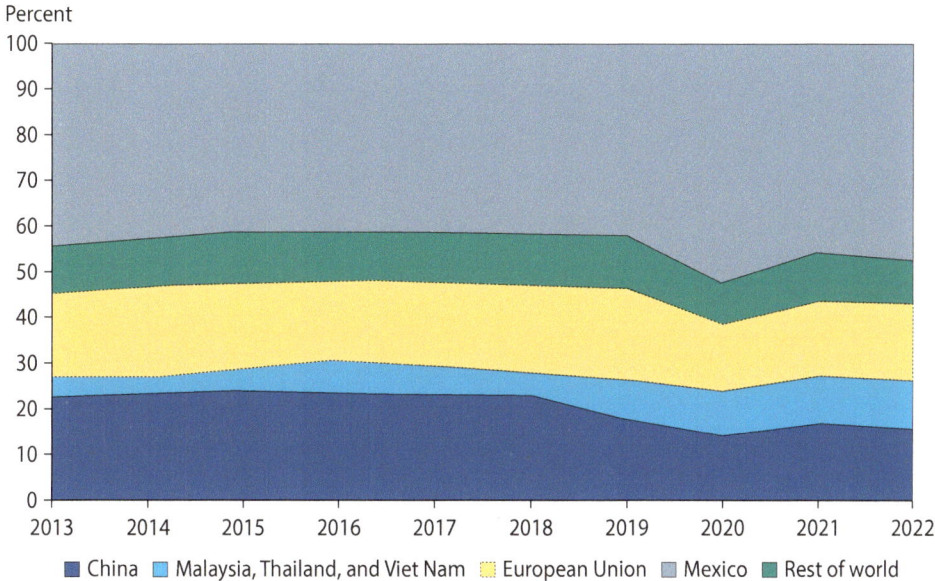

Source: Based on data from Base pour l'Analyse du Commerce International (BACI) (https://www.cepii.fr/CEPII/en/bdd _modele/bdd_modele_item.asp?id=37).

Effect of increasing participation in global green supply chains on diffusion of green technology at home

By participating in the global market for green products and services, EAP countries can pursue new growth opportunities while contributing to the worldwide diffusion of green technology. Capturing a larger share of global green supply chains does not automatically increase domestic adoption, however, as Malaysia's solar industry illustrates.

EAP countries can pursue new growth opportunities while contributing to the worldwide diffusion of green technology.

Following the imposition of anti-dumping tariffs on Chinese solar panels by the European Union and the United States in 2013 and 2014, Malaysia saw a significant increase in solar exports, driven by the rerouting of Chinese production to the country (Ratan 2023). Despite this scale-up in domestic production, local solar adoption did not seem to be affected: Proximity to solar manufacturers was not associated with increased solar installation among Malaysian firms. Qualitative evidence indicates that domestic production is geared primarily toward export markets, and Malaysian solar project owners continue to import more affordable panels from China. Barriers to broader solar adoption include limited demand, partly because of restrictions on exporting electricity, and financial constraints.

What factors affect demand for electric vehicles?

Adoption of electric vehicles (EVs) has gained speed as countries seek to reduce the carbon footprint of their transport sector. In 2023, almost one in five new vehicle sales was electric. Adoption is concentrated in China, Europe, and the United States, which together account for 95 percent of all EV sales (IEA 2024a).

Adoption paths have diverged significantly across countries. In China, the share of battery electric vehicles (BEVs) skyrocketed from less than 1 percent in 2015 to 25 percent of all new vehicle sales in 2022. This adoption rate was four times faster than in the United States, a much higher-income country and a pioneer in the industry. What explains such large differences in EV adoption, and what lessons can be drawn to facilitate the diffusion of EVs in emerging and developing economies?

Evidence from China, Germany, Norway, and the United States highlights the role of prices, government incentives, and consumer preferences in the adoption of EVs. In all markets, EV demand is highly sensitive to price (Li et al. 2017; Li et al. 2022; Remmy 2022; Springel 2021). Consumer subsidies therefore played a large role in increasing demand. Central and local government subsidies in China may have doubled the number of EVs there between 2015 and 2018 (Li et al. 2022). At the same time, there is evidence of significant heterogeneity in consumer preferences (Springel 2021). In both Germany and the United States, consumers prefer internal combustion engine (ICE) vehicles to EVs. As the attributes of EVs (such as driving range) improve, the inconvenience of purchasing them decreases (Gillingham et al. 2023; Remmy 2022).

Crucially, the market for EVs demonstrates strong network effects between EVs and charging infrastructure. Consumer demand for EVs increases with the availability of charging infrastructure, and charging station entry increases when adoption of EVs grows. As a result, government incentives that help expand the charging infrastructure are likely to be particularly effective in the early stage of the EV market, when EV sales are low and charging infrastructure underdeveloped (Li et al. 2017; Li et al. 2022; Springel 2021).

Differences in EV market structure across countries—attributable to factors such as the importance of incumbent ICE firms and the extent of national and subnational government support—also help explain differences in adoption patterns. Take the example of China and the United States: The United States was a pioneer in the EV industry but has not been as competitive as China. As of 2023, fewer than 20 firms competed in the US market, about half the number in China. More suppliers correspond to more choices and lower prices for consumers (refer to figures SF3.1.1 and SF3.1.2). In China, competitive cost reductions brought about cost parity between small EVs and conventional cars in 2022, providing a significant boost to EV demand.

FIGURE SF3.1.1   The up-front price gap between EVs and ICE vehicles has narrowed more in China than in the United States

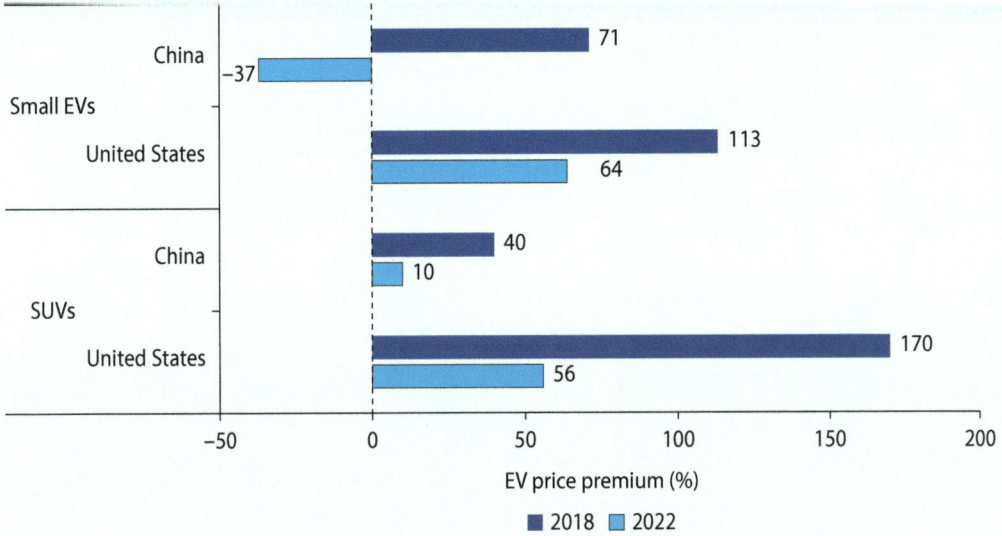

Source: IEA 2024a.
Note: EVs = electric vehicles; ICE = internal combustion engine; SUVs = sport utility vehicles.

FIGURE SF3.1.2   China's EV market offers consumers more choices than the US market

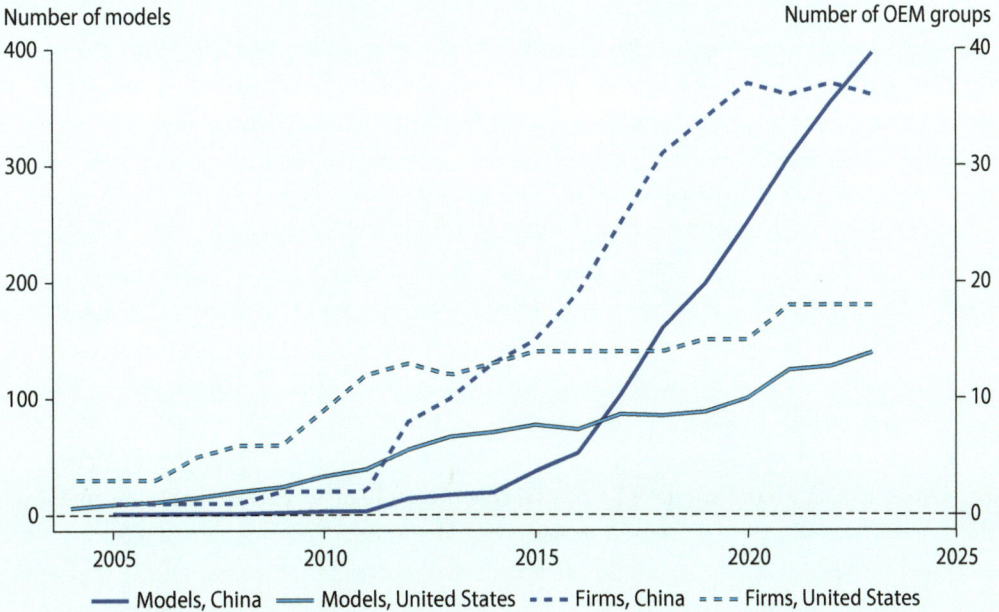

Source: Based on data from Marklines (https://www.marklines.com/en/).
Note: EV = electric vehicle; OEM = original equipment manufacturer.

FIGURE SF3.1.3   China has a denser EV charging network than the United States

Number of public charging points per EV

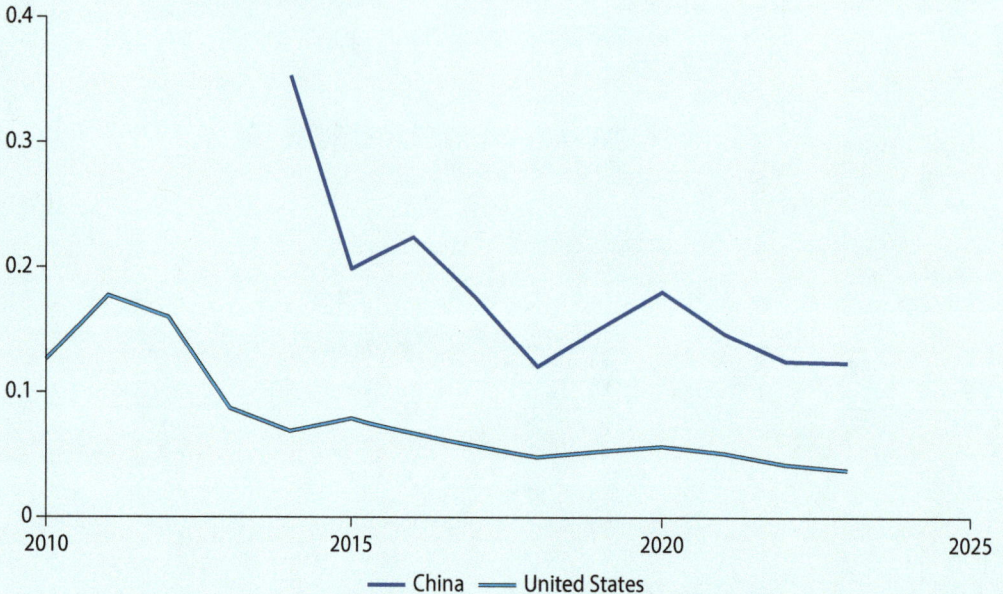

Source: Estimates using International Energy Agency data (https://www.iea.org/data-and-statistics/data-tools/global-ev-data-explorer).
Note: Charging points include both slow- and fast-charging stations. Electric vehicles (EVs) include battery EVs and plug-in hybrid EVs.

The total cost of ownership for EVs extends beyond the purchase price. It is affected by the cost of driving, which is determined by factors such as the availability of charging infrastructure and the relative prices of electricity and gasoline. China's extensive public charging network makes it cost-effective to operate EVs; in the United States, the lower density of charging stations hinders adoption (refer to figure SF3.1.3). States like California, where gasoline prices are higher relative to electricity costs than they are elsewhere in the United States, have seen higher EV penetration than in other states: In 2023, EVs accounted for more than a quarter of new car sales in California, the highest rate in the United States (Bui and Slowik 2024). Local differences in energy prices and infrastructure likely play a crucial role in determining the total cost of ownership of EVs and their potential for widespread adoption.

Government policy has also played a crucial role in shaping the market. As a latecomer in the automotive industry, the Chinese government identified EV technology as a priority in its Five-Year Plan in 2001, betting on the potential to succeed in this new market segment. As EVs are much simpler to produce than ICE vehicles (because they have fewer moving parts and a more compact powertrain), the advantage of historical carmakers is less pronounced in the EV market, making it easier for new entrants to capture market share (Yang 2023).

The Chinese government provided significant incentives to support the growth of domestic EV companies. Between 2009 and 2022, it allocated ¥200 billion (US$29 billion) in subsidies and tax breaks to the EV industry. In addition, local governments worked closely with EV companies to customize policies and support their growth, as exemplified by the partnership between BYD and the city of Shenzhen (Yang 2023). China's extensive supply chains and manufacturing capabilities provided a structural advantage, enabling the rapid scale-up of EV production. These factors contributed to the competition that helped drive down costs and improve product variety.

With the Inflation Reduction Act (IRA), US government support policy for EVs changed significantly. Before its passage, estimates suggested that China's central government spent five times more on EV purchase subsidies than the US government did between 2009 and 2022 (Bloomberg News 2023). Some projections indicate that the total fiscal costs of clean vehicle credits through 2031 could amount to US$390 billion (Bistline, Mehrotra, and Wolfram 2023). Since 2025, however, uncertainty has grown over the future of US government support for the EV industry, particularly regarding whether incentives will continue and how automakers will adapt to potential policy changes.

Notes

1. The staggering growth in patenting since the mid-2000s was not limited to green patents; the number of other patents from China also surged.
2. Looking at granted patents paints an almost identical picture, as roughly 75 percent of patent applications are granted.
3. The United States launched the China Initiative in November 2018, with the stated goal of preventing Chinese espionage. Only a small share of related judicial cases included charges of violating the Economic Espionage Act. The initiative increased administrative burden and reduced funding available for collaborating with Chinese researchers (Aghion et al. 2023).
4. Barwick et al. (2025) estimate that the battery industry has a learning rate of 18 percent and that learning-by-doing explained a substantial portion of the reductions in battery cost.
5. Support to BEV markets took the form of tax breaks, production subsidies, cheap land, loans, and grants (Bickenbach et al. 2024). Among China's A-shares companies, CATL was the largest recipient of subsidies, receiving almost ¥3 billion in the first half of 2023. SAIC Motor, BYD, and Chongqing Changan Automobile were also among the top 10 recipients of subsidies (company documents).
6. Although production in China is still cheaper than in Europe, India, or the United States, China's solar panel prices rose by 20 percent in 2021 because of high commodity prices and supply chain bottlenecks (IEA 2022b).
7. In the solar sector, part of this relocation was driven by Chinese firms' investing in Malaysia, Thailand, and Viet Nam (Ratan 2023).

References

Aghion, P., C. Antonin, L. Paluskiewicz, D. Stromberg, R. Wargon, K. Westin, and X. Sun. 2023. "Does Chinese Research Hinge on US Co-Authors? Evidence from the China Initiative." *LSE Research Online Documents on Economics* 121300. https://ideas.repec.org//p/ehl/lserod/121300.html.

Athreye, S., V. Kathuria, A. Martelli, and L. Piscitello. 2023. "Intellectual Property Rights and the International Transfer of Climate Change Mitigating Technologies." *Research Policy* 52 (9): 104819. https://doi.org/10.1016/j.respol.2023.104819.

Banares-Sanchez, I., R. Burgess, D. Laszlo, P. Simpson, J. V. Reenen, and Y. Wang. 2024. "Ray of Hope? Chinese Innovation, Green Industrial Policy and the Rise of Solar Energy." Unpublished paper. https://en.cafr.cn/Events/NBER/Ray%20of%20Hope%20China%20and%20the%20Rise%20of%20Solar%20Energy.pdf.

Barwick, P. J., H. S. Kwon, S. Li, and N. Zahur. 2025. "Drive Down the Cost: Learning by Doing and Government Policies in the Global EV Battery Industry." Working Paper 33378, National Bureau of Economic Research, Cambridge, MA. https://www.nber.org/papers/w33378.

Bickenbach, F., D. Dohse, R. J. Langhammer, and W. H. Liu. 2024. "Foul Play? On the Scale and Scope of Industrial Subsidies in China." Kiel Policy Brief 173, Kiel Institute for the World Economy, Kiel, Germany.

Bistline, J., N. Mehrotra, and C. Wolfram. 2023. "Economic Implications of the Climate Provisions of the Inflation Reduction Act." NBER Working Paper 31267, National Bureau of Economic Research, Cambridge, MA. https://doi.org/10.3386/w31267.

Bloomberg News. 2023. "From Cheap Cash to Tax Breaks, EVs in China Get Lots of Love." September 14, 2023. https://www.bloomberg.com/news/articles/2023-09-14 /from-cheap-money-to-tax-breaks-evs-in-china-get-a-lot-of-love.

BloombergNEF. 2025. "Energy Transition Investment Trends 2025: Tracking Global Investment in the Low-Carbon Energy Transition." https://assets.bbhub.io/professional /sites/24/951623_BNEF-Energy-Transition-Trends-2025-Abridged.pdf.

Bui, A., and P. Slowik. 2024. "Electric Vehicle Market and Policy Developments in US States, 2023." *ICCT20*, June 4. https://theicct.org/publication/ev-ldv-us -major-markets-monitor-2023-june24/.

Cao, Yu, F. de Nicola, A. Mattoo, and J. Timmis. 2024. "Technological Decoupling? The Impact on Innovation of US Restrictions on Chinese Firms." Policy Research Working Paper 10950, World Bank, Washington, DC. http://hdl.handle.net/10986/42282.

Carvalho, M., A. Dechezleprêtre, and M. Glachant. 2017. *Understanding the Dynamics of Global Value Chains for Solar Photovoltaic Technologies*, vol. 40. Geneva: World Intellectual Property Organization.

Corrocher, N., S. M. Grabner, and A. Morrison. 2024. "Green Technological Diversification: The Role of International Linkages in Leaders, Followers and Catching-Up Countries." *Research Policy* 53 (4): 104972. https://doi.org/10.1016/j.respol.2024.104972.

Curti, F., M. Macchiavelli, A. Mihov, and K. Pisciotta. 2023. "Stolen Secrets: The Effect of Trade Secret Theft on Corporate Innovation." SSRN Scholarly Paper 4613975. https://doi .org/10.2139/ssrn.4613975.

Dechezleprêtre, A., Y. Ménière, and M. Mohnen. 2017. "International Patent Families: From Application Strategies to Statistical Indicators." *Scientometrics* 111 (2): 793–828. https://doi.org/10.1007/s11192-017-2311-4.

Dussaux, D., A. Dechezleprêtre, and M. Glachant. 2022. "The Impact of Intellectual Property Rights Protection on Low-Carbon Trade and Foreign Direct Investments." *Energy Policy* 171: 113269. https://doi.org/10.1016/j.enpol.2022.113269.

Gillingham, K. T., A. A. van Benthem, S. Weber, M. A. Saafi, and X. He. 2023. "Has Consumer Acceptance of Electric Vehicles Been Increasing? Evidence from Microdata on Every New Vehicle Sale in the United States." *AEA Papers and Proceedings* 113: 329–35. https://doi .org/10.1257/pandp.20231065.

Green, M., and K. Stapleton. 2025. "Understanding Green Innovation in China." Unpublished paper, World Bank, Washington, DC, and Hertford College, University of Oxford.

IEA (International Energy Agency). 2021. *Patents and the Energy Transition*. Paris: IEA. https://www.iea.org/reports/patents-and-the-energy-transition.

IEA (International Energy Agency). 2022a. *Securing Clean Energy Technology Supply Chains*. Paris: IEA. https://iea.blob.core.windows.net/assets/0fe16228-521a-43d9-8da6 -bbf08cc9f2b4/SecuringCleanEnergyTechnologySupplyChains.pdf.

IEA (International Energy Agency). 2022b. *Special Report on Solar PV Global Supply Chains.* Paris: IEA. https://www.iea.org/reports/solar-pv-global-supply-chains.

IEA (International Energy Agency). 2022c. *Tracking Clean Energy Innovation in the Business Sector: An Overview.* Paris: IEA. https://www.iea.org/reports/tracking-clean -energy-innovation-in-the-business-sector-an-overview.

IEA (International Energy Agency). 2024a. *Global EV Outlook 2024.* Paris: IEA. https://www .iea.org/reports/global-ev-outlook-2024.

IEA (International Energy Agency). 2024b. *World Energy Investment 2024.* Paris: IEA. https://www.iea.org/reports/world-energy-investment-2024.

IMF (International Monetary Fund). 2022a. *Environmental Goods Trade Indicators Methodology.* https://climatedata.imf.org/documents/ad5179b954ed4a8389bf 6400324a901e/explore.

IMF (International Monetary Fund). 2022b. *Low Carbon Technology Products Trade Indicators Methodology.* https://climatedata.imf.org/documents/e46085cc97e445bb9c69e7 de3bffbbac/explore.

IMF (International Monetary Fund). 2024. *Fiscal Monitor: Fiscal Policy in the Great Election Year.* https://www.imf.org/en/Publications/FM/Issues/2024/04/17/fiscal-monitor-april-2024.

Li, S., L. Tong, J. Xing, and Y. Zhou. 2017. "The Market for Electric Vehicles: Indirect Network Effects and Policy Design." *Journal of the Association of Environmental and Resource Economists* 4 (1): 89–133. https://doi.org/10.1086/689702.

Li, S., X. Zhu, Y. Ma, F. Zhang, and H. Zhou. 2022. "The Role of Government in the Market for Electric Vehicles: Evidence from China." *Journal of Policy Analysis and Management* 41 (2): 450–85. https://doi.org/10.1002/pam.22362.

Martin, R., and D. Verhoeven. 2022. "Knowledge Spillovers from Clean and Emerging Technologies in the UK." *LSE Research Online Documents on Economics* 117804.

Maskus, K. E., and M. Penubarti. 1995. "How Trade-Related Are Intellectual Property Rights?" *Journal of International Economics* 39 (3): 227–48. https://doi.org /10.1016/0022-1996(95)01377-8.

Mealy, P., and A. Teytelboym. 2022. "Economic Complexity and the Green Economy." *Research Policy* 51 (8): 103948. https://doi.org/10.1016/j.respol.2020.103948.

Ratan, I. 2023. "Does Manufacturing Matter? Foreign Investment and Local Linkages in the Malaysian Solar Industry." https://ishanaratan.com/wp-content/uploads/2024/09/malaysia _paper_august2024-2-2.pdf.

Remmy, K. 2022. "Adjustable Product Attributes, Indirect Network Effects, and Subsidy Design: The Case of Electric Vehicles." CRC TR 224 Discussion Paper Series, article crctr224_2022_335, University of Bonn and University of Manheim, Germany. https:// ideas.repec.org//p/bon/boncrc/crctr224_2022_335.html.

Rosenow, S. K., and P. Mealy. 2024. "Turning Risks into Reward: Diversifying the Global Value Chains of Decarbonization Technologies." Policy Research Working Paper 10696, World Bank, Washington, DC. https://doi.org/10.1596/1813-9450-10696.

Springel, K. 2021. "Network Externality and Subsidy Structure in Two-Sided Markets: Evidence from Electric Vehicle Incentives." *American Economic Journal: Economic Policy* 13 (4): 393–432. https://doi.org/10.1257/pol.20190131.

Yang, Z. 2023. "How Did China Come to Dominate the World of Electric Cars?" https://www.technologyreview.com/2023/02/21/1068880/how-did-china-dominate-electric-cars-policy/.

Yang, Y., and M. Chen. 2017. "Toward a Sustainable Clean Energy Future: Lesson from Chinese Intellectual Property Litigations." Proceedings of the 2017 International Conference on Economics and Management, Education, Humanities and Social Sciences, Hangzhou, China. https://doi.org/10.2991/emehss-17.2017.32.

What determines the domestic diffusion of green technologies in East Asia and Pacific?

4

Green technology diffusion patterns in EAP

The diffusion of green technologies depends on their viability as well as local market conditions and the policy environment. Even when green technologies are in principle viable, their adoption can be hindered by policy distortions and market failures. And even when technologies are not yet viable, their diffusion can be induced by policies such as carbon taxes, which force firms and consumers to internalize the negative emission externalities.

China has been the pioneer in implementing green technology in developing East Asia (refer to figure 4.1). Renewable energy has gained market share and grown exponentially in several countries, such as China, Japan, the Republic of Korea, and Viet Nam. This rapid adoption coincides with the declining costs shown in chapter 3.

The diffusion of green technologies in East Asia generally follows their cost trajectories.

The surge in the deployment of renewables in China and Viet Nam and the adoption of battery electric vehicles (BEVs) in China have been particularly impressive (refer to figures 4.1 and 4.2). Between 2018 and 2020, the share of solar photovoltaic (PV) in total installed capacity in Viet Nam leaped from nearly zero to almost 25 percent, catching up to early adopters like Germany and Japan. In 2023, China accounted for more than half of global solar and wind installations, and BEVs accounted for a quarter of all new passenger vehicle sales in China (Bloomberg 2024). The share of BEVs within China's vehicle stock more than doubled in just two years, from 1.8 percent in 2020 to 4.9 percent in 2022.

Adoption of solar and wind power grew exponentially in several countries between 2000 and 2023.

FIGURE 4.1   Adoption of solar and wind power, selected countries, 2000–23

a. Solar

Share of total installed capacity (%)

b. Wind

Share of total installed capacity (%)

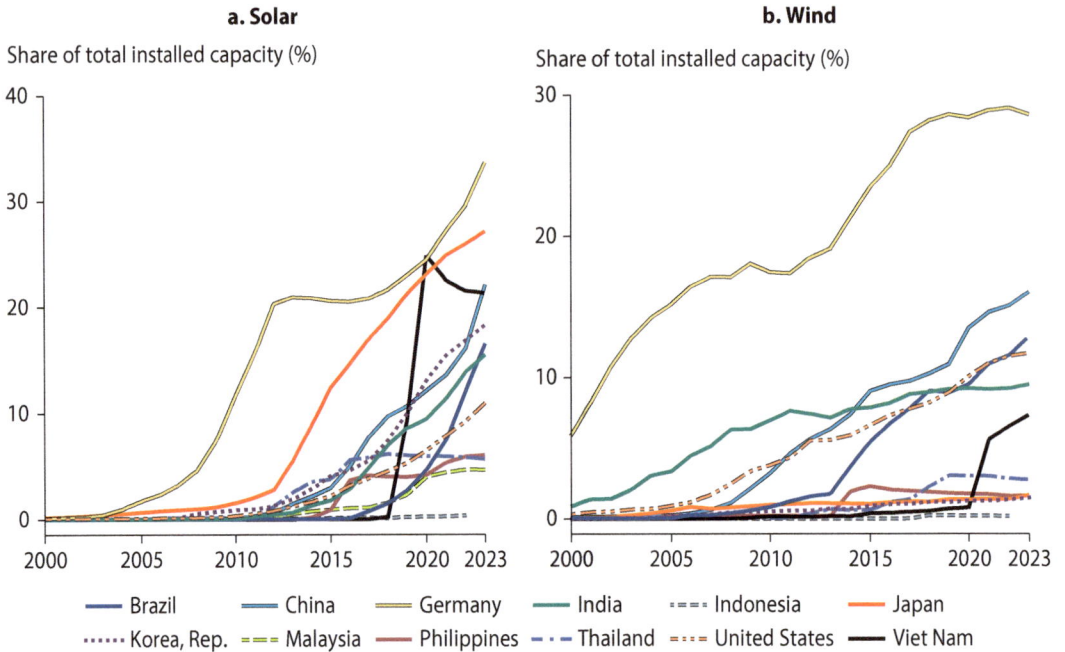

Brazil — China — Germany — India ⋯ Indonesia — Japan
⋯ Korea, Rep. === Malaysia — Philippines –·– Thailand ⋯ United States — Viet Nam

Source: Data from Ember (https://ember-energy.org/data/yearly-electricity-data/).

China and Europe dominate the market for BEVs.

FIGURE 4.2   Share of BEVs in total passenger vehicle stock, 2010–22

Percent

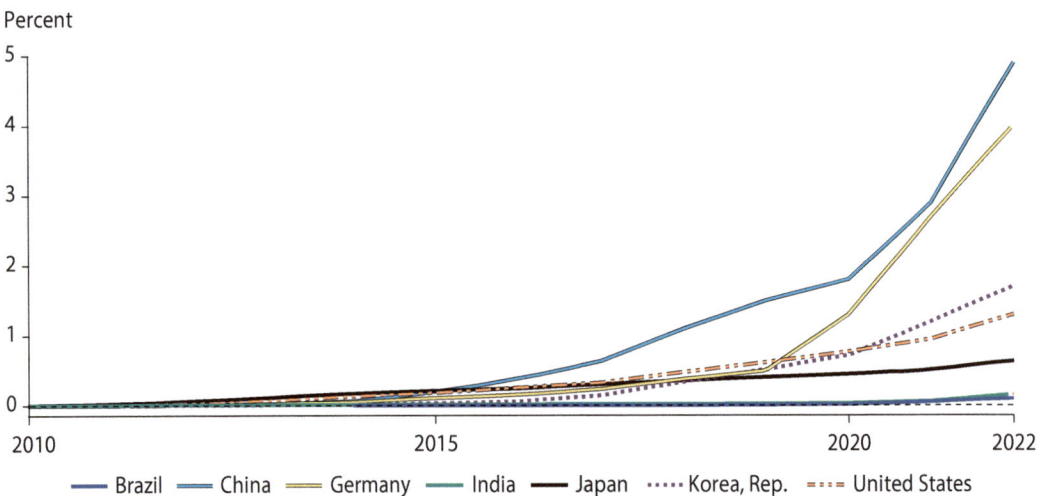

Brazil — China — Germany — India — Japan ⋯ Korea, Rep. === United States

Sources: Data from IEA 2024.
Note: BEVs = battery electric vehicles.

In contrast, technologies to decarbonize the industrial sector are at an early stage of diffusion and remain concentrated in high-income economies. East Asia and Pacific (EAP) countries except China have had limited adoption of these technologies. For example, within the region, green cement technology has not diffused outside of China even at the pilot or demonstration stages (refer to map 4.1). Malaysia and Thailand have a small amount of hydrogen capacity; China has built up significant capacity in hydrogen in recent years (refer to figure 4.3). Driven by China, the region had 70 percent of the world's installed electrolyzer capacity in 2022 (IEA 2023b). (Refer to special focus 4.1 at the end of this chapter for an overview of the uses and diffusion challenges for green hydrogen.)

The path of technology diffusion can also reverse—as it has in the steel industry, with the transition from the coal-based blast furnace–basic oxygen furnace (BF-BOF) technology to the electric arc furnace (EAF), which produces steel primarily from scrap using electricity. BF-BOF technology accounts for 70 percent of the world's steel production but more than 95 percent of the sector's emissions (Agora Industry and Wuppertal Institute 2023). In the near term, switching to EAF can provide significant reductions in carbon dioxide (CO_2) emissions from iron

> **Early-stage green technologies have seen limited diffusion in developing countries.**

MAP 4.1   Global uptake of green cement as of 2024

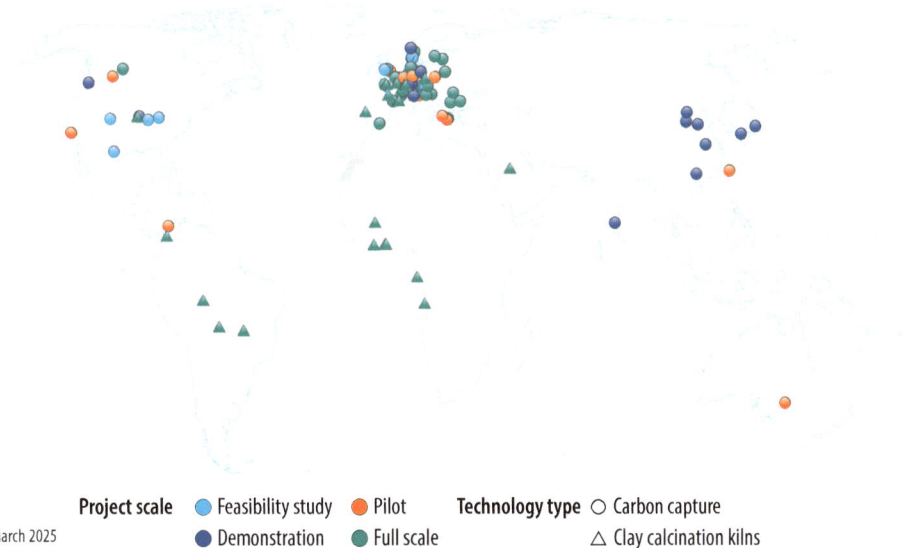

Project scale: Feasibility study, Pilot, Demonstration, Full scale   Technology type: ○ Carbon capture   △ Clay calcination kilns

IBRD 48762 | March 2025

Sources: Data from Leadership Group for Industry Transition, Green Cement Technology Tracker (Lorea, Sanchez, and Torres-Morales 2024; https://www.industrytransition.org/green-cement-technology-tracker/) and Natural Earth (https://www.naturalearthdata.com/downloads/110m-cultural-vectors/110m-admin-0-countries/).

Green hydrogen projects increased the most in China, Germany, Japan, and the United States from 2000 to 2022.

FIGURE 4.3 **Green hydrogen projects, 2000–22**

Log announced capacity (MWel)

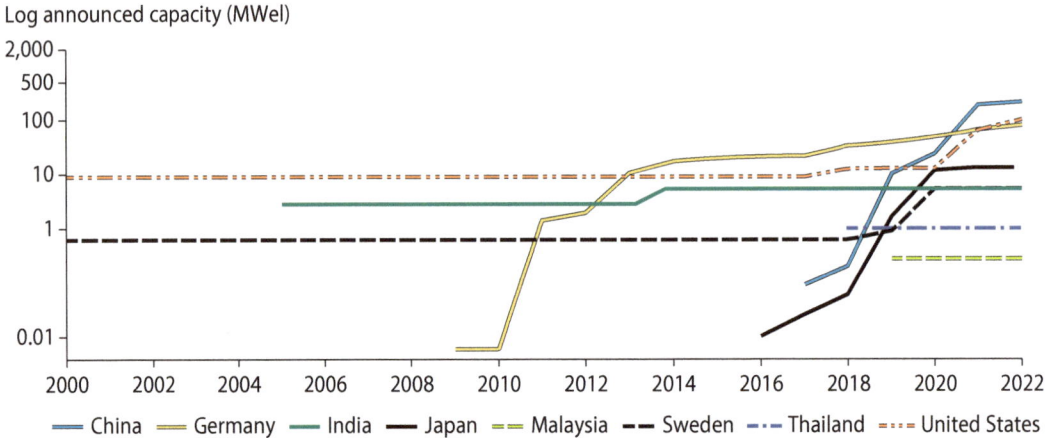

Source: International Energy Agency, Hydrogen Production and Infrastructure Projects Database, November 2022 version (https://www.iea.org/data-and-statistics/data-product/hydrogen-production-and-infrastructure-projects-database).
Note: The figure includes only projects under construction or operational and with estimated capacity. Cumulative capacity plotted in log scale. MWel = megawatts of electricity input.

and steel production (Jaramillo et al. 2023). The two technologies are not perfect substitutes, however, as EAF has lower productivity for certain products. It became cheaper than BF-BOF in recent years (refer to figure 4.4, panel a) and gained dominance in high-income economies such as the United States. Its lower fixed cost also allows adoption in lower-income countries. Despite these advantages, Indonesia and Viet Nam have seen a reverse in the use of EAF (refer to figure 4.4, panel b), driven by rising steel demand. As the gap in quality between steel produced using the two processes narrows because of technological advancements in EAF processes, the relative viability of EAF may yet improve in the future.

Significant differences in adoption patterns across countries illustrate the importance of barriers to adoption that are specific to a region or country context. A technology that is cost-competitive globally may not be viable locally because of differences in factor endowments (such as the abundance of coal reserves or sunshine), industrial structure, and/or market or policy distortions (such as fossil fuel subsidies).

Diffusion patterns vary widely across countries, reflecting differences in local viability.

The path of technology diffusion may reverse.

FIGURE 4.4   Relative cost and capacity of steel production, by EAF technology

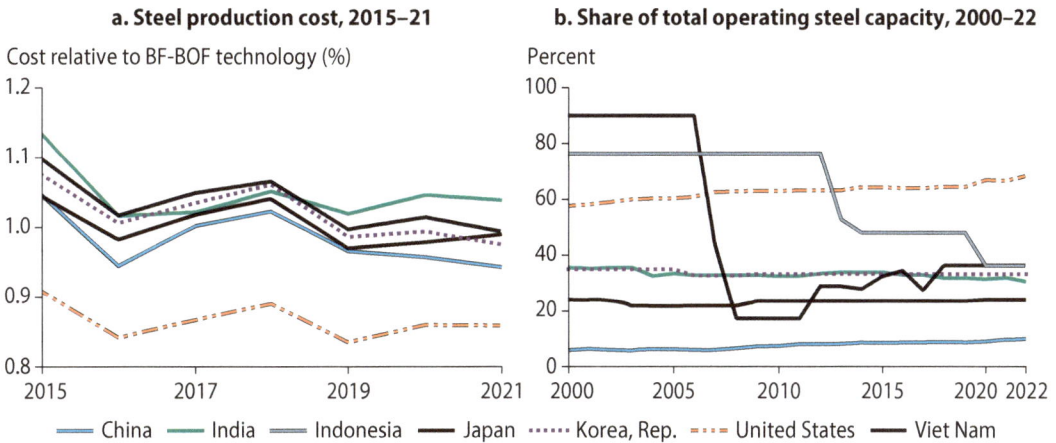

a. Steel production cost, 2015–21

b. Share of total operating steel capacity, 2000–22

Legend: China, India, Indonesia, Japan, Korea, Rep., United States, Viet Nam

Source: Data from the Global Steel Cost Tracker (https://www.transitionzero.org/products/global-steel-cost-tracker).
Note: In panel a, cost data is not available for Indonesia. BF-BOF = blast furnace–basic oxygen furnace; EAF = electric arc furnace.

Effect of market and policy distortions on domestic diffusion

Economic distortions that artificially lower the costs of conventional energy sources, raise the cost of green technologies, or increase the cost of complementary inputs may prevent otherwise viable green technologies from being adopted. These distortions include fossil fuel subsidies,[1] entry barriers that favor carbon-intensive technologies, investment and trade restrictions, market or policy failures affecting the labor and financial markets, and network externalities and coordination failures affecting enabling infrastructure.

Energy market distortions

The EAP region has implemented policies that explicitly or implicitly support the use of fossil fuels. In Indonesia, for instance, the government has committed to an excess buildup of coal-based power plants through long-term power purchase agreements, making it expensive to switch to cleaner energy sources (Hamdi and Adhiguna 2021). Explicit fossil fuel subsidies as a share of gross domestic product (GDP) in EAP increased steadily from 0.13 percent in 2015 to 1.63 percent in 2022 (IMF 2023). These subsidies penalize green alternatives by making fossil fuel–based investments more attractive. Analysis of greenfield foreign direct investment (FDI) projects suggests that investments in renewables decrease with fuel subsidies in investment destinations and that the effect in EAP is significantly larger than the global average (refer to figure 4.5). When energy subsidies are cut, firms improve their energy efficiency by replacing fuel-powered equipment with more efficient electric alternatives (Calì et al. 2022).

> **Energy market distortions in EAP increase the profitability of dirty technologies.**

> **Foreign investments in renewables decrease with fuel subsidies in investment destinations.**

FIGURE 4.5   Impact of fuel subsidies on foreign investments in renewable energy, EAP and all countries, 2011–20

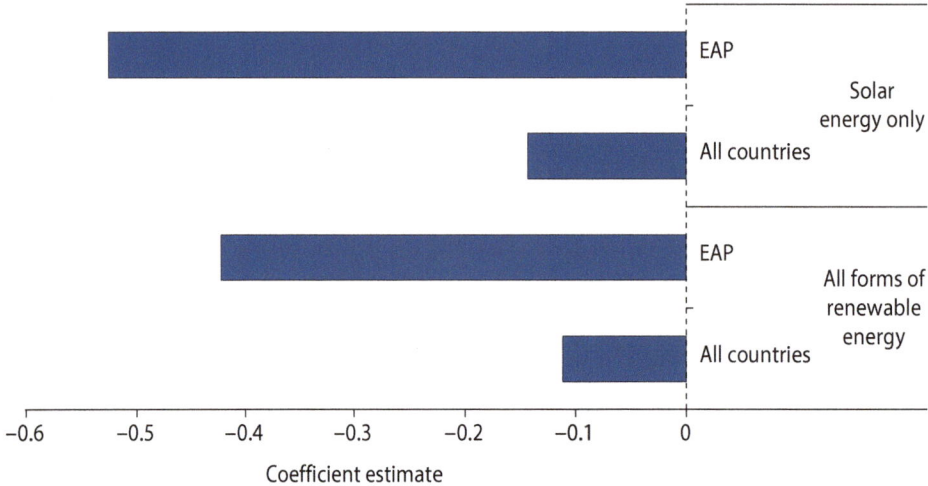

Sources: Data on the number of bilateral greenfield foreign direct investment projects in the renewable sector were constructed using data from fDiMarkets (https://www.ftlocations.com/products-and-services/fdi-markets). Data on fuel subsidies are from the International Monetary Fund fuel subsidies database (https://www.imf.org/-/media/Files/Topics/energy-subsidies/EXTERNALfuelsubsidiestemplate2023new.ashx).

Note: Figures are coefficient estimates from a Poisson pseudo maximum likelihood model on greenfield projects in renewables to account for many country pairs with no bilateral investments. Results on bilateral greenfield foreign direct investment projects in the renewable sector are qualitatively similar but less precise using investment amounts. Results control for the stock of patents in the investor's country and fuel subsidies in the destination country. The stock of patents is the cumulative number of patents in each sector (solar, onshore, offshore wind) in the source (investor) country. Lagged fuel subsidies indicate the previous year's fuel subsidies as a share of GDP. The final sample includes data for 2011–20. Results are similar when controlling for the stock of patents in both origin and destination countries; origin country fixed effects; destination country fixed effects; and other gravity variables (GDP, difference in GDP, distance, common language, contiguity, common colony). EAP = East Asia and Pacific.

Even temporary fuel subsidies can create a lock-in effect. With imperfect financial markets, firms may not adjust their technologies in periods with higher energy costs because of capital adjustment costs. In the United States, for example, firms entering the market when energy prices are low tend to have higher energy intensity throughout their lifetime (Hawkins-Pierot and Wagner 2023).

Structural market distortions also impede the adoption of green technologies. No country in EAP except the Philippines has a real-time national balancing market that allows market participants to engage in intertemporal arbitrage (IFC 2020). In China, the absence of economic dispatch prevents zero-marginal-cost renewables from receiving priority access to the grid, leading to curtailment and reduced profitability (World Bank 2022). Lack of pricing flexibility has dampened incentives for providers of energy storage to fully utilize China's large battery capacity (Bloomberg 2023).

Investment and trade policy distortions

Globally, FDI has been a significant source of financing for the deployment of green technologies, especially in the renewable energy sector. Estimates based on project-level data from fDiMarkets suggest that total greenfield FDI in renewable energy reached US$80 billion in 2021, close to a quarter of worldwide investment in renewable energy in that year (BloombergNEF 2023). In EAP, FDI in the solar sector is positively correlated with the diffusion of solar energy in the region (refer to figure 4.6).

FDI and trade facilitate the diffusion of technology.

FDI is important not only because it provides capital but also because it serves as a conduit for knowledge about green technologies, as foreign firms tend to have cleaner technologies and processes than their domestic counterparts. In Spain, for example, average environmental expenditures are higher for foreign-owned firms (Balaguer, Cuadros, and García-Quevedo 2023). In Viet Nam, foreign-owned firms

---

Diffusion of solar energy increases with the stock of greenfield foreign direct investment in solar in EAP.

FIGURE 4.6   Foreign direct investment and diffusion of solar energy in EAP

ln (Installed capacity per million inhabitants, MW)

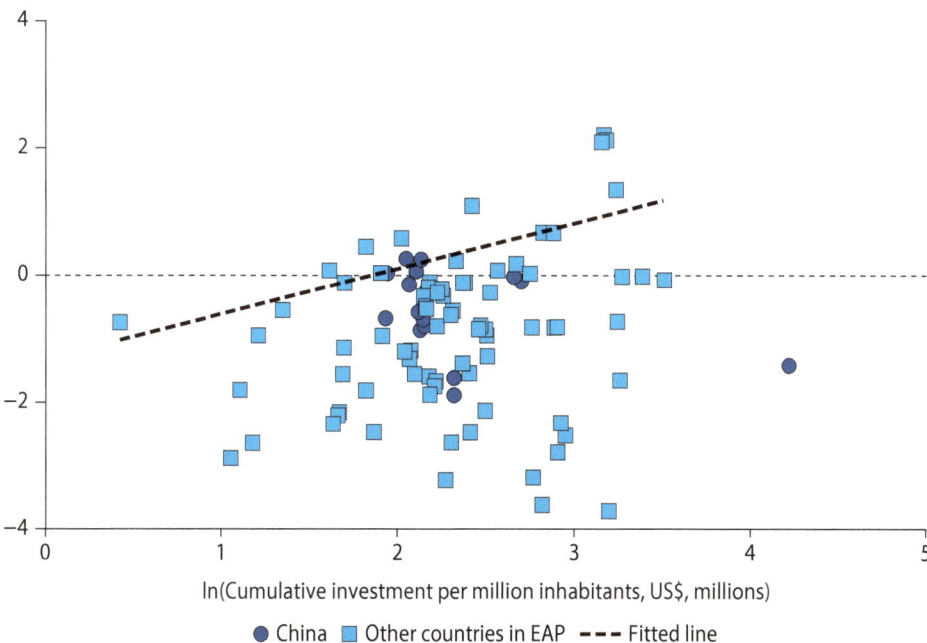

ln(Cumulative investment per million inhabitants, US$, millions)

● China   ■ Other countries in EAP   - - - Fitted line

Sources: Data from fDiMarkets (https://www.ftlocations.com/products-and-services/fdi-markets) and International Renewable Energy Agency (https://www.irena.org/Data).
Note: Results control for country and year fixed effects. EAP = East Asia and Pacific; MW = megawatts.

have significantly lower energy and emission intensities than domestic firms of similar size in the same sectors (refer to figure 4.7). In Indonesia, the energy intensity of otherwise similar manufacturing plants declines by 30 percent after foreign acquisitions, driven by improved process efficiency rather than changes in the output mix (Brucal, Javorcik, and Love 2019).

Trade provides an avenue for the rapid transfer of technology embedded in imported products and for learning by exporting. Although the extent to which trade promotes the diffusion of green technologies has not been firmly established, there is evidence of a correlation between trade activities and green innovation capabilities. In Colombia, for example, export activities are strongly associated with process and product innovations to reduce water and energy consumption by manufacturing firms (Castillo and Vonortas 2024). Regions in the European Union with higher values of backward participation in global value chains (that is, regions that import more intermediate goods for exports) tend to have more green patents per capita (Colozza, Pietrobelli, and Vezzani 2024).

> **In Viet Nam, foreign-owned firms of similar asset size are less energy intensive than their domestic counterparts.**

FIGURE 4.7   Energy intensity, by firm ownership and asset size, Viet Nam, 2016

Energy intensity (log energy consumption/VA output)

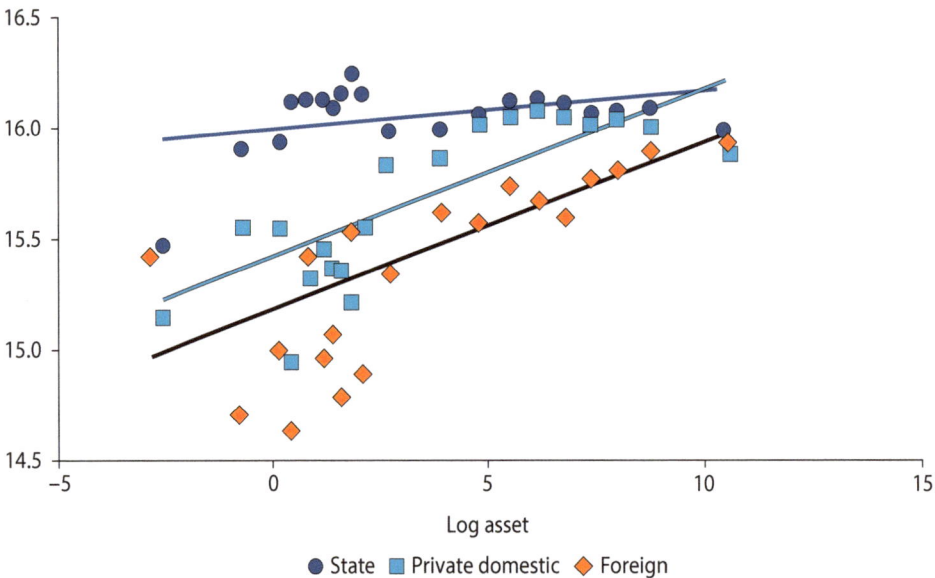

Source: Data from the Viet Nam Enterprise Survey.
Note: Binned scatterplots of energy intensity by firm asset size in 2016. Data include all sectors except utilities. Figures are conditional on four-digit sector fixed effects. VA = value added.

Amidst the recent rise in trade tensions, EAP significantly ramped up the use of discriminatory trade and investment measures targeting low-carbon technology (LCT) goods (refer to figure 4.8). These restrictions could potentially impede the flow of green technologies. Globally, firm-level imports of environmental goods tend to decrease with tariff barriers (Rosenow, Espitia, and Fernandes 2024). The transfer of climate mitigation technologies—as measured by the cross-border transfer of patents—decreases with tariffs and capital market controls (Dechezleprêtre, Glachant, and Ménière 2013).

Trade and FDI policy restrictions can distort trade and investment flows, raising the cost of green technologies.

FDI and trade barriers such as local content requirements (LCRs) may help promote domestic industries and employment, but they tend to deter investors and raise short-term costs when domestic manufacturing capacity is limited (OECD 2015). In India, for example, where domestically produced solar panels were 14 percent more expensive than imported ones, LCRs for public solar PV auctions are estimated to have increased generation costs by 6 percent between 2014 and 2017 (Probst et al. 2020). In East Asia, Indonesia currently has one of the world's most extensive systems of LCRs in the renewable energy sector (IRENA 2022a). This policy has been blamed for the slow uptake of solar, as developers struggle to meet stringent LCRs in the face of weak local manufacturing capacity (WEF 2022).

> **EAP countries introduced many discriminatory trade and investment measures against LCT goods between 2018 and 2022.**

FIGURE 4.8   Trade and investment interventions affecting LCT goods, EAP, 2009–22

Number of newly introduced measures

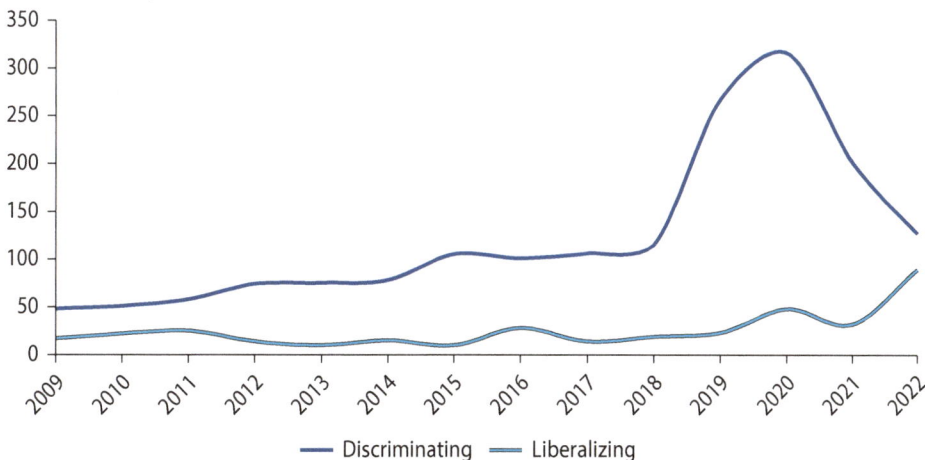

Discriminating — Liberalizing

Source: Data from the Global Trade Alert database (https://globaltradealert.org/data-center).
Note: EAP = East Asia and Pacific; LCT = low-carbon technology.

Trade policy can also lead to green goods being disproportionately taxed when they cross borders (refer to figure 4.9). In most countries, tariffs and nontariff barriers (NTBs) are substantially lower for upstream industries than for downstream industries (Shapiro 2021). Because upstream industries tend to emit more CO_2 per unit of output, most countries end up imposing higher tariffs on cleaner goods. As a result, global emissions increase. The impact of this bias is estimated to be similar in magnitude to that of some of the world's largest actual or proposed climate change policies (Shapiro 2021). Although this trade policy bias is less pronounced in EAP countries than elsewhere in the world, the region still imposes higher NTBs on clean industries than on dirtier ones.

Trade barriers introduced amid US–China tensions are reallocating trade and production, with potential spillover impacts that extend well beyond their borders. These barriers likely affect the flows of green goods and technologies. Tariffs on China's exports to the United States have increased substantially since 2017 for all goods, including LCT goods (refer to figure 4.10). The tariff hike correlates with a significant downturn in US imports from China (refer to figure 4.11).

Trade tensions between China and the United States can have opposing effects on technology diffusion and carbon emissions.

Globally, trade policy is biased against cleaner goods.

FIGURE 4.9   Nontariff barriers and products' CO_2 intensity

Nontariff barrier ad valorem rate (%)

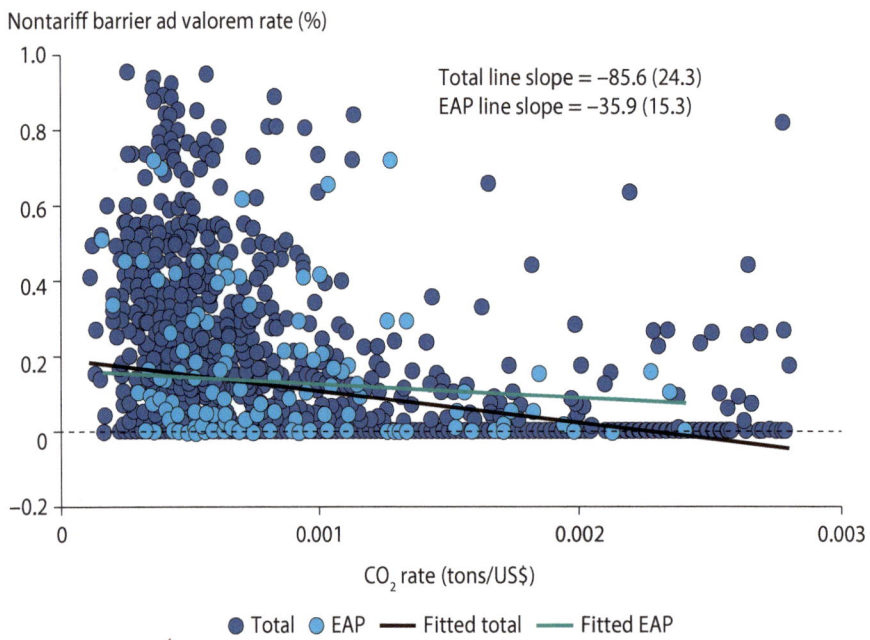

Total line slope = −85.6 (24.3)
EAP line slope = −35.9 (15.3)

CO_2 rate (tons/US$)

● Total   ● EAP   ━━ Fitted total   ━━ Fitted EAP

Source: Shapiro 2021.
Note: Each dot represents a sector. CO_2 = carbon dioxide; EAP = East Asia and Pacific.

Initial evidence indicates a corresponding reshuffling of production along global value chains (Alfaro and Chor 2023; Freund et al. 2023). A diversion of production out of China could have mixed consequences for the diffusion of green technologies and emissions for other countries in EAP and globally, for several reasons.

US tariffs on Chinese goods increased significantly in 2018 and 2019, especially on LCT goods.

FIGURE 4.10   Changes in US tariffs on Chinese imports, 2018 and 2019 relative to 2017

Average change in tariffs (%)

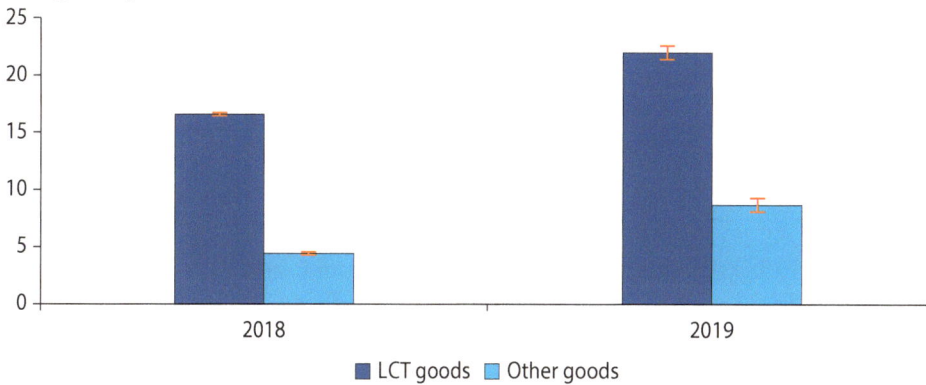

Source: Data from Fajgelbaum et al. 2024.
Note: Changes shown are relative to 2017. Error bars show 95 percent confidence intervals. LCT = low-carbon technology.

US imports from China dropped significantly after the tariff hike in 2018.

FIGURE 4.11   Change in China's market share of US imports, 2012–22

Market share change (%)

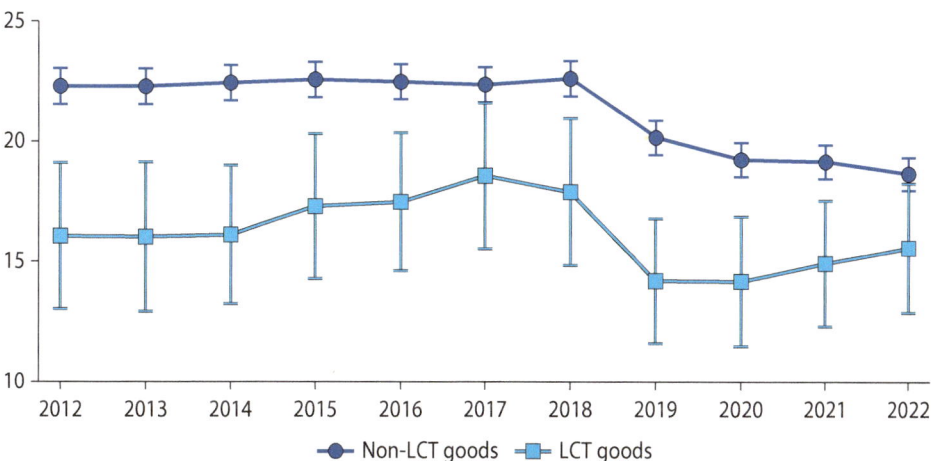

Source: Bilateral trade data from Base pour L'Analyse du Commerce International (BACI) (https://www.cepii.fr/CEPII/en/bdd _modele/bdd_modele_item.asp?id=37).
Note: Error bars show 95 percent confidence intervals. LCT = low-carbon technology.

First, shifting production out of China risks increasing total emissions if China uses green technologies more intensively than other countries. Research by Dang, Krishna, and Zhao (2024) using US import data illustrates the potential emissions costs of the current trade reallocation. Using the same measure of industry dirtiness as Shapiro (2021), they show that new tariffs disproportionately affected goods that China can produce more cleanly than other countries. As a result, the estimated emission intensity associated with US imports increased by 0.4 percent on average between 2015 and 2019.

Second, trade diversion from China could reduce the short-term costs of importing green technologies for third countries. The increasing share of LCT goods from China, especially intermediate and capital goods, underscores China's growing role as a green technology supplier in the region (refer to figure 4.12). As trade tensions redirect China's exports, other EAP countries could see lower import prices.

> **The rest of EAP has increasingly sourced solar products from China.**

FIGURE 4.12   Share of EAP imports of products in the solar value chain from China, 2000–22

Share of imports (%)

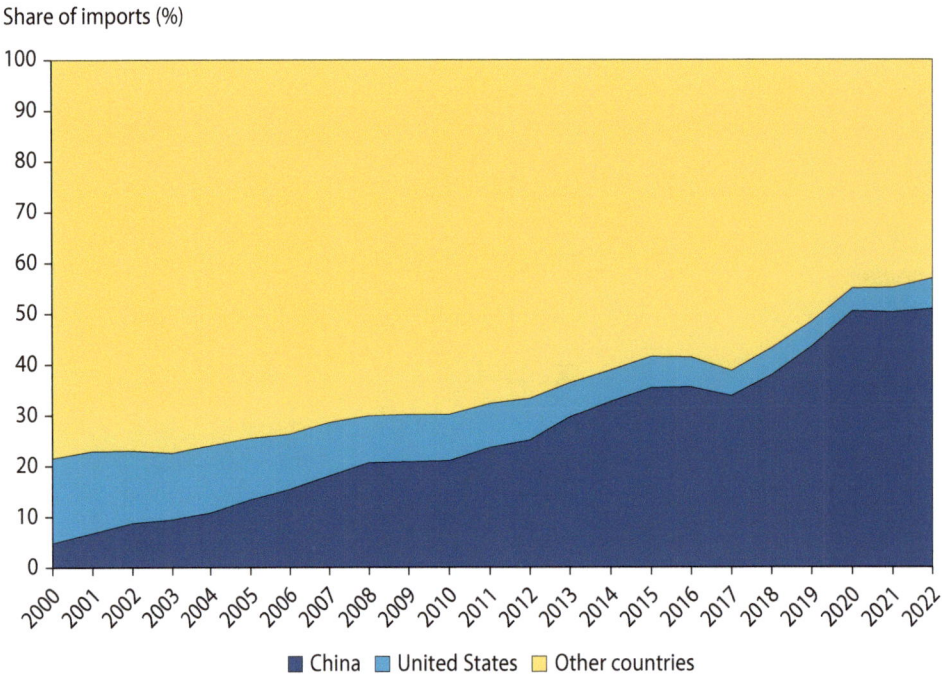

Source: Bilateral trade data from Base pour L'Analyse du Commerce International (BACI) (https://www.cepii.fr/CEPII/en/bdd_modele/bdd_modele_item.asp?id=37).
Note: Goods in the solar value chain are defined as in Rosenow and Mealy (2024).

> **When China exports less to the United States, import prices of LCT goods decline in other EAP countries.**

FIGURE 4.13   **Impact of declines in China's exports to the United States on import prices of LCT goods in other EAP countries, 2017–22**

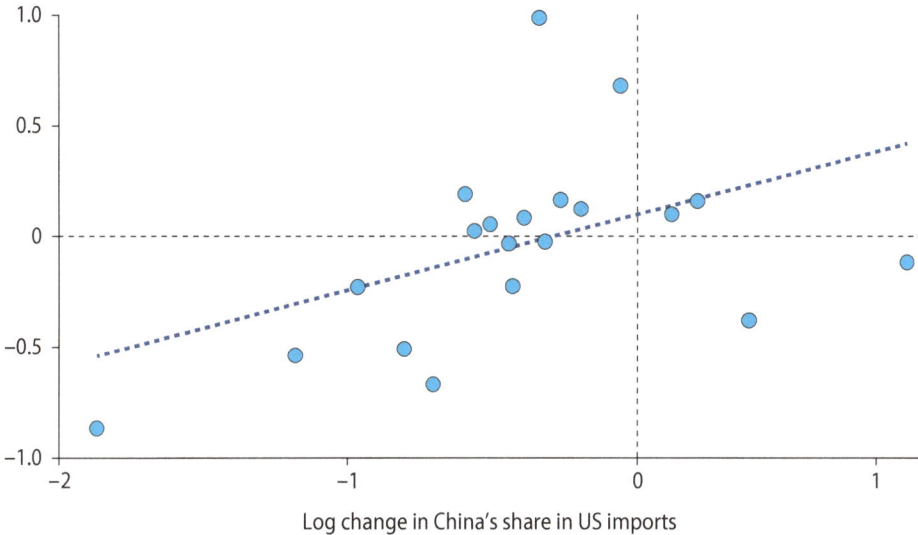

Log change in import unit value

Log change in China's share in US imports

Source: Bilateral trade data from Base pour L'Analyse du Commerce International (BACI), 2017–22. (https://www.cepii.fr /CEPII/en/bdd_modele/bdd_modele_item.asp?id=3).
Note: Each dot indicates a country. LCT goods are goods that produce less pollution than their traditional energy counterparts. They include wind turbines, solar panels, biomass systems, and carbon capture equipment. Classification is based on Pigato et al. (2020). EAP = East Asia and Pacific; LCT = low-carbon technology.

Initial data support this link: As China's LCT exports to the United States decrease, the cost for EAP countries to import these goods from China tends to drop (refer to figure 4.13). This dynamic suggests that shifts in trade patterns, particularly those that reduce the volume of China's exports to the United States, could make it more cost-effective for EAP countries to adopt LCTs in the near term. The long-term implications of such a shift in production are not fully understood. Chapter 6 discusses the potential spillover effects of policy decisions in high-income countries for the region.

Lack of needed skills

The cost of adopting green technologies depends in part on the availability of complementary skills, which in turn depends on the extent to which the required skill profiles differ substantially from existing ones. There is some indication that green skills differ from nongreen skills along several dimensions. First, as most green

Because of coordination failures and adjustment costs, demand for complementary skills may outpace supply.

technologies are still at an early stage, their adoption likely requires higher-skilled workers and managers. Firm-level evidence suggests that Chinese firms with highly educated chief executive officers are more likely than other Chinese firms to engage in environmental innovation, especially if they operate in regions with strict environmental regulations (Zhou, Chen, and Chen 2021).

Second, the set of tasks involved may be different. Examining skills used more intensively in green occupations in the United States, Vona et al. (2018) identify two core skill sets that distinguish green jobs: (1) engineering skills for designing and producing clean technologies, and (2) managerial skills for setting up and monitoring environmental organizational practices.

The supply of green skills may be slow to adapt to demand because of coordination failures, information asymmetries about skill demand, relocation costs, and other labor market frictions. There is very little evidence on the extent to which the labor market is responding to the changing skills demand from green technologies in the region. However, indicative data from LinkedIn job postings worldwide provide some evidence of a growing global mismatch. Between 2016 and 2021, global job postings requiring green skills grew at an annual rate of 8 percent, while the share of workers with green skills grew by just 6 percent.[2] The growth in demand for green skills accelerated between 2022 and 2023, with the share of job postings requiring at least one green skill increasing by 22 percent. In contrast, the share of workers with green skills grew at only half that rate, at 12 percent (LinkedIn Economic Graph 2022, 2023).

Mismatches between supply and demand and job losses in dirty industries can create political costs for the green transition. Job losses often have a scarring effect, with displaced workers earning significantly less than they did before displacement, even years after being laid off (Hanson 2023). Concentrated job losses in specific local labor markets or among disadvantaged workers may be politically unacceptable, further delaying the transition. In China, green jobs and existing fossil fuel jobs are geographically disparate: Fossil fuel jobs are concentrated in Shanxi, and new demand for green jobs, as measured by online job advertisements, is concentrated in eastern cities (Park et al. 2024). The human cost of these mismatches needs to be addressed through social protection and active labor market policies, which can soften the pain of transition and equip workers with relevant new skills.

High up-front costs

Financial frictions can lead to underinvestment in green technologies when they are embedded in durable assets that require large up-front costs. Lanteri and Rampini (2025) show how collateral constraints cause a range of firms with limited internal funds to choose dirty

> **High up-front costs lead financially constrained firms to underinvest in green technologies.**

technologies even when the per unit user cost of green technologies is lower. They find that larger shipping fleets operate with higher energy efficiency than smaller ones, by investing in cleaner new technologies and operating newer capital, which tends to be more energy efficient.[3] Similar patterns are evident among manufacturing firms in Indonesia (Doarest and Tran 2022). Larger firms—measured in revenue or employment—exhibit lower energy and emissions intensity than smaller firms. They also report a significantly higher probability of investing in new equipment to reduce energy consumption or carbon emissions.

These results imply that higher levels of financial development not only increase the overall level of investment but also influence its composition, favoring green technology adoption. De Haas and Popov (2023) provide consistent evidence across a large number of countries and industries that carbon-intensive industries transition more rapidly to the use of low-carbon production technologies in economies with deeper stock markets.

Credit supply shocks may disproportionately affect green investments. De Haas et al. (2024) find that green investments are negatively correlated with credit constraints and that the credit crunch following the global financial crisis led to long-lasting increases in firms' carbon intensity and total emissions.

Cost of capital

Other market and policy distortions can deter green technology investments by increasing the risk premium required. New technologies, including green ones, often face significant information asymmetries because of investors' limited experience with them. Uncertainty about the paths of emerging technologies may also be more pervasive than

Market and policy distortions raise the cost of capital for green technologies.

it is for established technologies. Policy uncertainty poses additional risks, because of potential changes in the relative profitability of green versus dirty technologies. As a result, investors may demand higher returns to compensate for the elevated risks associated with green technologies, driving up the cost of capital.[4] The high cost of capital partly explains the outsize role of the public sector in green financing (Climate Policy Initiative 2022).

Whether investors and lenders overestimate the risks of green technologies is an empirical question. Giraudet, Petronevich, and Faucheux (2021) find mixed evidence in France. They find patterns consistent with efficient loan pricing for green vehicle loans. But they also find that banks charge higher interest rates for green than for conventional home retrofits, despite similar default rates.

> Cost of capital accounts for a much higher share of the levelized cost of electricity in less developed markets.

FIGURE 4.14   Composition of levelized cost of electricity for a utility-scale solar PV plant with final investment decision secured, selected countries, 2021

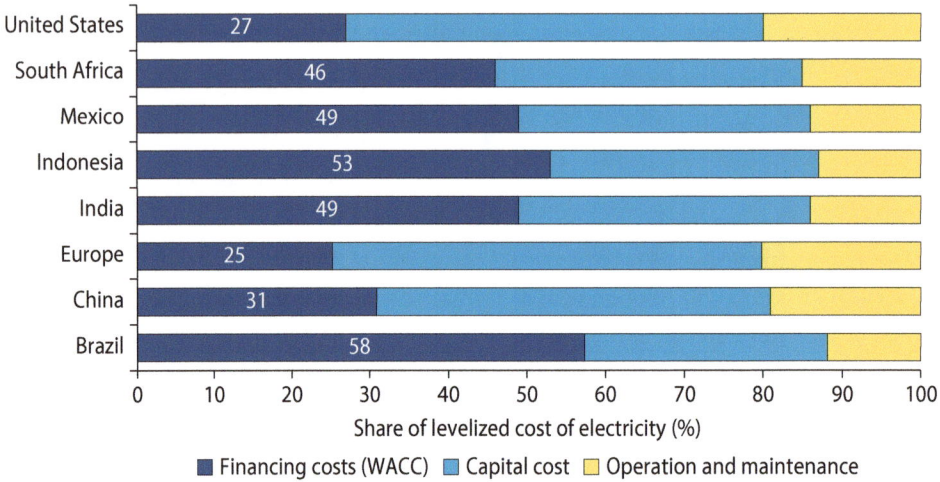

Source: Internatinal Energy Agency, Cost of Capital Observatory (https://www.iea.org/data-and-statistics/data-tools/cost-of-capital-observatory).
Note: PV = photovoltaic; WACC = weighted average cost of capital (including cost of debt and equity).

Policy distortions contribute to disproportionately higher costs of capital in less developed markets. Estimates by the International Energy Agency (IEA) show that financing accounts for 53 percent of the total levelized cost of electricity for a typical utility-scale solar PV plant in Indonesia—more than twice the rate in Europe (refer to figure 4.14). Survey results reveal that political and regulatory risks are among the top factors driving higher financing costs. Uncertainties around issues such as permitting, offtake agreements, and adverse regulatory changes increase the risk premiums demanded. Addressing these policy-related risks—by establishing a more predictable regulatory framework, for example—can improve the viability of green technologies. Difficult-to-address risks also motivate the use of blended finance (the blending of public and philanthropic capital) to subsidize private investment.

Importance of complementary infrastructure

The adoption of green technology hinges on the availability of complementary infrastructure. The intermittent nature of renewable technologies requires a flexible grid infrastructure to smooth fluctuations through solutions such as energy storage, expanded transmission, demand management, and backup generation.

> The availability of complementary inputs is critical to the demand for green technologies.

Modeling results from Ziegler et al. (2019) illustrate this complementarity: For renewables to become cost-competitive enough to provide 100 percent of US energy, energy storage costs need to decrease by 90 percent.[5] Evidence from household consumption patterns reaches a similar conclusion. Twenty percent of US households that adopted solar and storage would not have adopted solar power had storage not been available (Bollinger et al. 2024).

Electric vehicle (EV) technologies exhibit similar complementarities. In China, Germany, Norway, and the United States, EV demand increases as the network of charging stations expands and vice versa (Li et al. 2017; Li et al. 2022; Remmy 2022; Springel 2021). Because of such network effects, coordination failures can lead to underinvestment in enabling infrastructure, inhibiting the diffusion of green technologies (Popp 2019).

Need for more and better grid technologies

Nearly three-quarters of total carbon emissions come from fossil fuel energy use. Electrification is therefore a centerpiece of global decarbonization efforts (Rapson and Bushnell 2024). Without an expanded transmission grid that can accommodate the new demand for electricity that will replace fossil fuels with renewables, the world's green transition will be severely constrained.

This expansion requires the adoption of new grid technologies, such as high-voltage direct current transmission lines and flexible alternating current transmission systems to enhance the efficiency and reliability of long-distance power transmission. Smart-grid technologies—including advanced metering infrastructure; distributed energy resources (such as EVs, solar panels, and home batteries); and demand response programs—will also play a role in balancing supply and demand, ensuring grid stability and flexibility.

The integration of intermittent renewables and distributed energy resources into larger energy markets can enhance investment incentives. Conversely, transmission congestion undermines them, as seen in the United States, where long queues and high interconnection costs led many wind and solar developers to withdraw their investments (Johnston, Liu, and Yang 2023). In EAP, the surge in renewable energy capacity without adequate grid upgrades resulted in substantial curtailment. In China, renewable curtailment reached 16 percent in 2012 and 2016 (refer to figure 4.15). In Viet Nam's Ninh Thuan and Binh Thuan provinces, solar farms were forced to operate at 30–50 percent of capacity because of congested transmission grids, even as the country's coal-dependent northern provinces faced supply challenges (Urakami 2023; Vu 2024). A survey of solar developers reveals that weak grid capacity is considered the most critical barrier to new investment (Urakami 2023).

> **China has reduced its renewable energy curtailment problem.**

FIGURE 4.15   VRE technical curtailment rate in China, 2011–22

Technical curtailment rate (%)

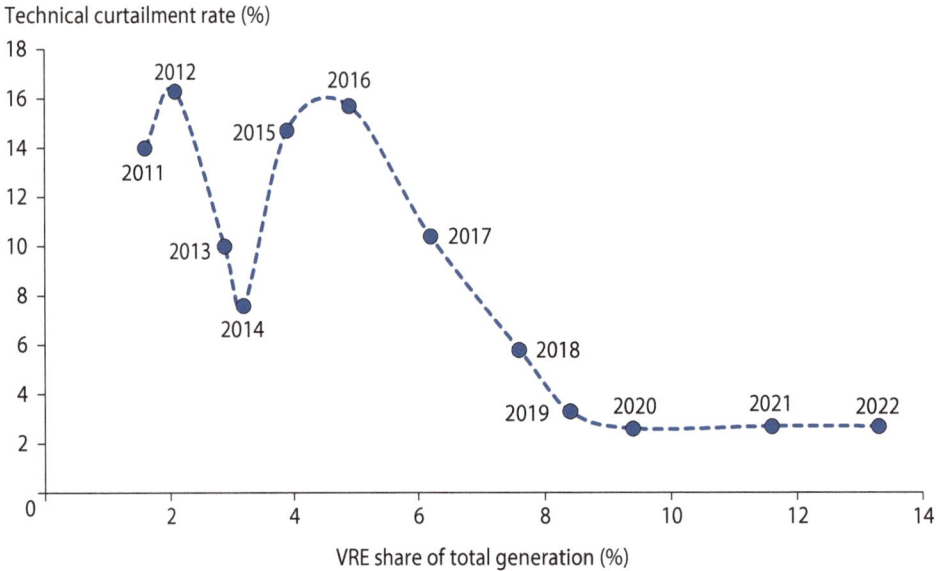

VRE share of total generation (%)

Source: Data from IEA 2023a.

Note: VRE is defined here as solar PV and wind. Technical curtailment refers to the dispatch-down of renewable energy because of network or system reasons. PV = photovoltaic; VRE = variable renewable energy.

The scale of the challenge to expand and modernize the grid is enormous. The IEA projects that the world needs to construct over 80 million kilometers of grid by 2040 to meet current national climate goals, essentially doubling existing global grid infrastructure in 2022. China reduced curtailment in recent years with large-scale investment in transmission infrastructure and grid digitalization (refer to figure 4.15). Investments in emerging markets outside of China are low, however (IEA 2023a).

It is difficult to find comparable measures of the grid's readiness to accommodate future growth in renewable energy, but cross-country regulatory indicators suggest that EAP countries outside of China are lagging in system planning and providing incentives for renewable energy integration (refer to figure 4.16). The widest gaps compared with other high-income countries and best practices lie in renewable grid integration, which involves improving grid flexibility, enabling renewable energy participation in grid support services markets, using forecasting, and implementing real-time grid management to effectively integrate variable renewable energy sources.

China leads the world in renewable energy integration planning and incentives, while other EAP countries lag the rest of the world.

FIGURE 4.16   Regulatory score for renewable energy integration planning and incentives, EAP, Europe, and the United States, 2021

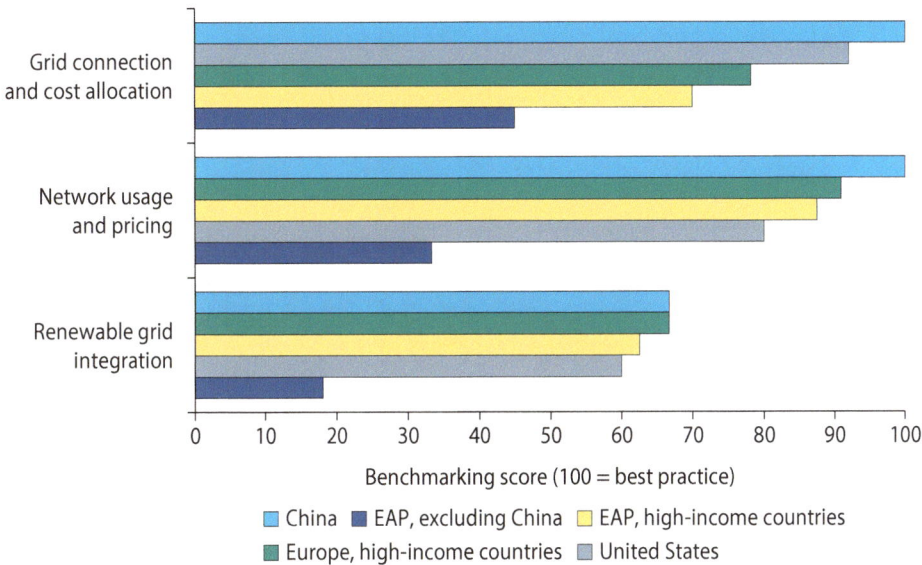

Source: Data from the Regulatory Indicators for Sustainable Energy database (https://rise.esmap.org/scoring-system).
Note: EAP = East Asia and Pacific.

Need to enhance coordination

Coordination failures and related governance issues likely pose the most significant challenge to achieving the scale and speed needed for the transition to net-zero emissions. Policy frameworks for a green transition need to move beyond regulations and incentives at the level of individual technologies or industries to long-term planning for system-level transformation. Starting the transition early is crucial, because of the long time required to establish institutions capable of overcoming these challenges. Several countries (Australia, Canada, Ireland, the Philippines, and the United Kingdom) have created dedicated institutions, such as climate change commissions and similar bodies, to help coordinate transition efforts across different sectors and levels of government.

How promising is "green" hydrogen?

Hydrogen can be produced in several ways. "Gray" hydrogen is produced through a process that uses a catalyst to facilitate a reaction between methane and high-temperature steam, resulting in hydrogen, carbon monoxide, and a small amount of carbon dioxide (CO_2). The CO_2 and impurities are removed, leaving pure hydrogen. Propane, gasoline, and coal use this production process. "Blue" hydrogen is produced in a similar process, except that the CO_2 produced from the steam methane reforming process is captured and stored elsewhere. "Green" hydrogen is produced through water electrolysis powered by renewable energy that splits water into hydrogen and oxygen.

The emergence of green hydrogen solutions offers a promising avenue for reducing emissions in traditionally challenging sectors. Hydrogen is a highly versatile energy source. It can be used to generate heat; store energy; and produce steel, ammonia, and plastics.

Green hydrogen is not yet economically viable, but it is potentially competitive relative to alternative technologies in certain areas. Hydrogen has higher energy density and becomes more valuable when converted to a derivative, such as methanol or synthetic fuels.

Figure SF4.1.1 shows green hydrogen's use cases and their potential competitiveness. Converting green hydrogen into ammonia is considered one of the more promising clean options for producing fertilizers and powering maritime transport. Conversely, the use of green hydrogen as a fuel for small passenger vehicles is not likely to be competitive with existing technologies such as battery electric vehicles.

Lower renewable energy costs are a necessary but not sufficient condition for competitive green hydrogen production. Reducing the cost of electrolysis facilities (the second-largest cost component) can help. The International Renewable Energy Agency (IRENA 2020) identifies strategies to do so, including optimizing the design and construction of electrolyzers, exploiting economies of scale, and avoiding using hard-to-procure materials. However, equipment and financial costs are increasing, jeopardizing viability. Green hydrogen projects are capital intensive: The International Energy Agency (IEA 2023c) estimates that a 3 percentage point increase in the cost of capital raises the total project cost by almost a third.

After a slow start, China is expanding electrolyzer deployment. In 2020, China was involved mostly in small demonstration projects, accounting for less than 10 percent of the global installed capacity of electrolyzers for hydrogen production. In 2022, installed capacity grew to more than 200 megawatts, or 30 percent of the global capacity. By 2023, China had become a global leader in installed capacity, with cumulative capacity of 0.8 gigawatts (GW) (almost 60 percent of global capacity) and 9 GW under final investment decision or under construction (IEA Hydrogen Production and Infrastructure Projects Database [https://www.iea.org/data-and-statistics/data-product/hydrogen-production-and-infrastructure-projects-database]).

The competitiveness of hydrogen varies with use cases.

FIGURE SF4.1.1 **The Hydrogen Ladder: Use cases for hydrogen and their competitiveness, 2023**

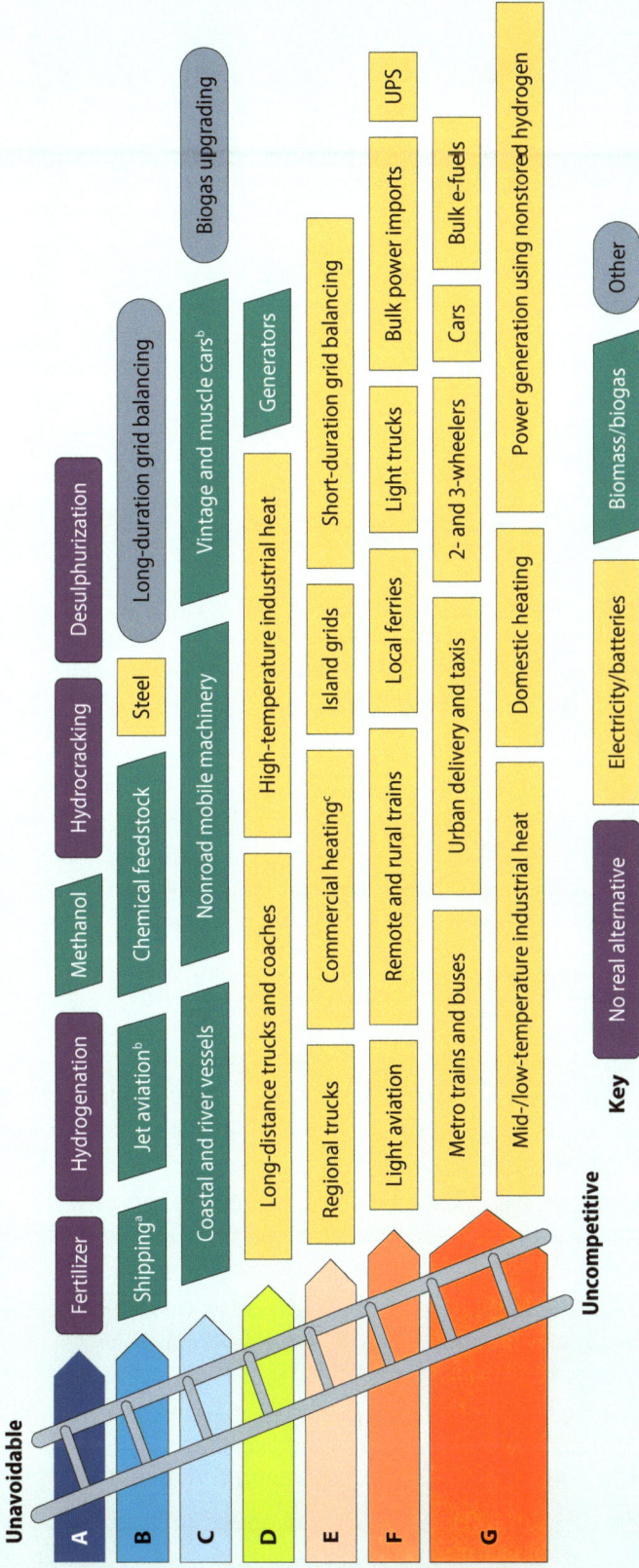

Unavoidable

A — Fertilizer | Hydrogenation | Methanol | Hydrocracking | Desulphurization

B — Shipping[a] | Jet aviation[b] | Chemical feedstock | Steel | Long-duration grid balancing

C — Coastal and river vessels | Nonroad mobile machinery | Vintage and muscle cars[b]

D — Long-distance trucks and coaches | High-temperature industrial heat | Generators

E — Regional trucks | Commercial heating[c] | Island grids | Short-duration grid balancing

F — Light aviation | Remote and rural trains | Local ferries | Light trucks | Bulk power imports | UPS

G — Metro trains and buses | Urban delivery and taxis | 2- and 3-wheelers | Cars | Bulk e-fuels

Mid-/low-temperature industrial heat | Domestic heating | Power generation using nonstored hydrogen

Uncompetitive

Key

No real alternative | Electricity/batteries | Biomass/biogas | Other

Source: Liebreich 2023. Used with permission.

Note: Use cases are ranked from A to G, from closest to farthest from market. UPS = uninterruptible power supply.

a. As ammonia or methanol.

b. As e-fuel or power and biomass to liquid.

c. As hybrid system.

Notes

1.   See Damania et al. (2023) for a detailed discussion on how subsidy reform can help safeguard the world's foundational natural assets—clean air, land, and oceans.
2.   Workers are considered to have green skills if they cite green skills in their profile and/or work in a job that is relatively intense in green skills.
3.   This pattern can also be consistent with economies of scale, however.
4.   The cost of capital (or financing cost) expresses the expected financial return, or the minimum required rate, for investing in a company or a project. This expected return is closely linked with the degree of risk associated with a company or project cash flows.
5.   The model assumes a system that would precisely match supply to demand, providing baseload, intermediate, and peaking power, given real-world resource availability conditions, every hour of every day, over 20 years.

References

Agora Industry, and Wuppertal Institute. 2023. *15 Insights on the Global Steel Transformation.* https://www.agora-industry.org/publications/15-insights-on-the-global-steel-transformation.

Alfaro, L., and D. Chor. 2023. "Global Supply Chains: The Looming 'Great Reallocation.'" NBER Working Paper 31661, National Bureau of Economic Research, Cambridge, MA. https://doi.org/10.3386/w31661.

Balaguer, J., A. Cuadros, and J. García-Quevedo. 2023. "Does Foreign Ownership Promote Environmental Protection? Evidence from Firm-Level Data." *Small Business Economics* 60 (1): 227–44. https://doi.org/10.1007/s11187-022-00646-1.

Bloomberg. 2023. "China Solar and Storage Firms Face Challenging 2024: BNEF Summit." November 27. https://www.bloomberg.com/news/articles/2023-11-27/china -s-energy-path-in-focus-ahead-of-cop28-bnef-summit-update.

Bloomberg. 2024. "China Added More Solar Panels in 2023 Than US Did in Its Entire History." January 26. https://www.bloomberg.com/news/articles/2024-01-26/china -added-more-solar-panels-in-2023-than-us-did-in-its-entire-history.

BloombergNEF. 2023. "Energy Transition Investment Trends 2023: Tracking Global Investment in the Low-Carbon Energy Transition." https://assets.bbhub.io/professional /sites/24/energy-transition-investment-trends-2023.pdf.

Bollinger, B., N. Darghouth, K. Gillingham, and A. Gonzalez-Lira. 2023. "Valuing Technology Complementarities: Rooftop Solar and Energy Storage." NBER Working Paper 32003, National Bureau of Economic Research, Cambridge, MA. https://doi.org/10.3386/w32003.

Brucal, A., B. Javorcik, and I. Love. 2019. "Good for the Environment, Good for Business: Foreign Acquisitions and Energy Intensity." *Journal of International Economics* 121: 103247. https://doi.org/10.1016/j.jinteco.2019.07.002.

Calì, M., N. Cantore, L. Iacovone, M. Pereira-López, and G. Presidente. 2022. "Too Much Energy: The Perverse Effect of Low Fuel Prices on Firms." *Journal of Environmental Economics and Management* 111: 102587. https://doi.org/10.1016/j.jeem.2021.102587.

Castillo, J. C., and N. S. Vonortas. 2024. "Firm-Level Determinants of Eco-innovation Strategies in Colombia." Unpublished manuscript.

Climate Policy Initiative. 2022. *Global Landscape of Climate Finance: A Decade of Data.* San Francisco. https://www.climatepolicyinitiative.org/publication/global-landscape -of-climate-finance-a-decade-of-data/.

Colozza, F., C. Pietrobelli, and A. Vezzani. 2024. "Do Global Value Chains Spread Knowledge and Pollution? Evidence from EU Regions." *Journal of Cleaner Production* 444: 141180. https://doi.org/10.1016/j.jclepro.2024.141180.

Damania, R., E. Balseca, C. De Fontaubert, J. Gill, K. Kim, J. Rentschler, J. Russ, and E. Zaveri. 2023. *Detox Development: Repurposing Environmentally Harmful Subsidies.* Washington, DC: World Bank. https://doi.org/10.1596/978-1-4648-1916-2.

Dang, H., K. Krishna, and Y. Zhao. 2024. "Global Reallocations of Environmentally Related Goods and Dirty Goods as a Result of the US-China Trade War." Working paper.

De Haas, R., R. Martin, M. Muûls, and H. Schweiger. 2024. "Managerial and Financial Barriers to the Green Transition." *Management Science,* ahead of print, June 26, 2024. https://doi.org/10.1287/mnsc.2023.00772.

De Haas, R., and A. Popov. 2023. "Finance and Green Growth." *Economic Journal* 133 (650): 637–68. https://doi.org/10.1093/ej/ueac081.

Dechezleprêtre, A., M. Glachant, and Y. Ménière. 2013. "What Drives the International Transfer of Climate Change Mitigation Technologies? Empirical Evidence from Patent Data." *Environmental and Resource Economics* 54 (2): 161–78. https://doi.org/10.1007 /s10640-012-9592-0.

Doarest, A., and T. Tran. 2022. "Greening Manufacturing Firms in Indonesia: Evidence from Microdata." Background paper for 2023 Indonesia Country Climate and Development Report, World Bank, Washington, DC.

Fajgelbaum, P., P. Goldberg, P. Kennedy, A. Khandelwal, and D. Taglioni. 2024. "The US-China Trade War and Global Reallocations." *American Economic Review: Insights* 6: 295–312. https://doi.org/10.1257/aeri.20230094.

Freund, C., A. Mattoo, A. Mulabdic, and M. Ruta. 2023. "Is US Trade Policy Reshaping Global Supply Chains?" Policy Research Working Paper 10593, World Bank, Washington, DC. https://doi.org/10.1596/1813-9450-10593.

Giraudet, L.-G., A. Petronevich, and L. Faucheux. 2021. "Differentiated Green Loans." *Energy Policy* 149: 111861. https://doi.org/10.1016/j.enpol.2020.111861.

Hamdi, E., and P. Adhiguna. 2021. "Indonesia Wants to Go Greener, but PLN Is Stuck with Excess Capacity from Coal-Fired Power Plants." Institute for Energy Economics and Financial Analysis, Cleveland, OH. https://ieefa.org/wp-content/uploads/2021/11 /Indonesia-Wants-to-Go-Greener-but-PLN-Is-Stuck-With-Excess-Capacity_November -2021.pdf.

Hanson, G. H. 2023. "Local Labor Market Impacts of the Energy Transition: Prospects and Policies." NBER Working Paper 30871, National Bureau of Economic Research, Cambridge, MA. https://www.nber.org/system/files/working_papers/w30871/w30871.pdf.

Hawkins-Pierot, J. T., and K. R. H. Wagner. 2023. "Technology Lock-In and Costs of Delayed Climate Policy." https://www.krhwagner.com/papers/carbon_lockin.pdf.

IEA (International Energy Agency). 2023a. *Electricity Grids and Secure Energy Transitions.* Paris: IEA. https://www.iea.org/reports/electricity-grids-and-secure-energy-transitions.

IEA (International Energy Agency). 2023b. *Energy Technology Perspectives 2023.* Paris: IEA. https://www.iea.org/reports/energy-technology-perspectives-2023.

IEA (International Energy Agency). 2023c. "Lagging Policy Support and Rising Cost Pressures Put Investment Plans for Low-Emissions Hydrogen at Risk" (blog), September 22, 2023. https://www.iea.org/news/lagging-policy-support-and-rising-cost-pressures-put-investment -plans-for-low-emissions-hydrogen-at-risk/.

IEA (International Energy Agency). 2024. *Global EV Outlook 2024.* Paris: IEA. https://www .iea .org/reports/global-ev-outlook-2024.

IFC (International Finance Corporation. 2020. The Power Market Database. Washington, DC. https://www.worldbank.org/en/who-we-are/ifc/power-markets-database.

IMF (International Monetary Fund). 2023. Fuel Subsidies Database. Washington, DC. https://www.imf.org/-/media/Files/Topics/energy-subsidies/EXTERNALfuelsubsidies template2023new.ashx.

IRENA (International Renewable Energy Agency). 2020. *Green Hydrogen Cost Reduction.* Masdar City, United Arab Emirates: IRENA. https://www.irena.org/publications/2020/Dec /Green-hydrogen-cost-reduction.

IRENA (International Renewable Energy Agency). 2022a. *Renewable Energy Auctions*: *Southeast Asia.* Masdar City, United Arab Emirates: IRENA. https://www.irena.org /Publications/2022/Dec/Renewable-energy-auctions-Southeast-Asia.

IRENA (International Renewable Energy Agency). 2022b. *Renewable Power Generation Costs in 2021.* Masdar City, United Arab Emirates: IRENA. https://www.irena.org /publications/2022/Jul/Renewable-Power-Generation-Costs-in-2021.

Jaramillo, P., V. J. Karplus, P. C. Pistorius, and E. Severnini. 2023. "The Costs and Distributional Impacts of Decarbonizing the Iron and Steel Industry in the United States." Technical report. https://conference.nber.org/conf_papers/f176895.pdf.

Johnston, S., Y. Liu, and C. Yang. 2023. "An Empirical Analysis of the Interconnection Queue." NBER Working Paper 31946, National Bureau of Economic Research, Cambridge, MA. https://doi.org/10.3386/w31946.

Lanteri, A., and A. A. Rampini. 2025. "Financing the Adoption of Clean Technology." NBER Working Paper 33545, National Bureau of Economic Research, Cambridge, MA. https://doi.org/10.3386/w33545.

Li, S., L. Tong, J. Xing, and Y. Zhou. 2017. "The Market for Electric Vehicles: Indirect Network Effects and Policy Design." *Journal of the Association of Environmental and Resource Economists* 4 (1): 89–133. https://doi.org/10.1086/689702.

Li, S., X. Zhu, Y. Ma, F. Zhang, and H. Zhou. 2022. "The Role of Government in the Market for Electric Vehicles: Evidence from China." *Journal of Policy Analysis and Management* 41 (2): 450–85.

Liebreich, M. 2023. "Clean Hydrogen Ladder." Version 5.0. Liebreich Associates, London.

LinkedIn Economic Graph. 2022. *Global Green Skills Report 2022.* https://linkedin.github.io /global-green-report-2022/.

LinkedIn Economic Graph. 2023. *Global Green Skills Report 2023.* https://economicgraph .linkedin.com/content/dam/me/economicgraph/en-us/global-green-skills-report/green-skills -report-2023.pdf.

Lorea, C., F. Sanchez, and E. Torres-Morales. 2024. "Green Cement Technology Tracker." May 2024. Stockholm: Leadership Group for Industry Transition. https://www.industrytransition.org/green-cement-technology-tracker.

OECD (Organisation for Economic Co-operation and Development). 2015. *Local-Content Requirements in the Solar- and Wind-Energy Global Value Chains*. Paris: OECD Publishing. https://doi.org/10.1787/9789264227064-6-en.

Park, G., A. Shen, K. Wang, L. Yang, and K. Stapleton. 2024. "The New Geography of Low Carbon Technology Jobs in China." Background paper, Country Climate and Development Report for China. World Bank, Washington, DC.

Pigato, M. A., S. J. Black, D. Dussaux, Z. Mao, M. McKenna, R. Rafaty, and S. Touboul. 2020. *Technology Transfer and Innovation for Low-Carbon Development*. International Development in Focus. Washington, DC: World Bank.

Popp, D. 2019. "Environmental Policy and Innovation: A Decade of Research." NBER Working Paper 25631, National Bureau of Economic Research, Cambridge, MA. https://doi.org/10.3386/w25631.

Probst, B., V. Anatolitis, A. Kontoleon, and L. D. Anadón. 2020. "The Short-Term Costs of Local Content Requirements in the Indian Solar Auctions." *Nature Energy* 5 (11): 842–50. https://doi.org/10.1038/s41560-020-0677-7.

Rapson, D., and J. Bushnell. 2024. "The Limits and Costs of Full Electrification." *Review of Environmental Economics and Policy* 18 (1): 26–44. https://doi.org/10.1086/728927.

Remmy, K. 2022. "Adjustable Product Attributes, Indirect Network Effects, and Subsidy Design: The Case of Electric Vehicles." CRC TR 224 Discussion Paper Series, article crctr224_2022_335, University of Bonn and University of Manheim, Germany. https://ideas.repec.org/p/bon/boncrc/crctr224_2022_335.html.

Rosenow, S., A. Espitia, and A. Fernandes. 2024. "High Tariffs, High Stakes: The Policy Drivers behind Firm-Level Adoption of Green Technologies." Policy Research Working Paper 10977, World Bank, Washington, DC. http://hdl.handle.net/10986/42453.

Rosenow, S. K., and P. Mealy. 2024. "Turning Risks into Reward: Diversifying the Global Value Chains of Decarbonization Technologies." Policy Research Working Paper 10696, World Bank, Washington, DC. https://doi.org/10.1596/1813-9450-10696.

Shapiro, J. S. 2021. "The Environmental Bias of Trade Policy." *Quarterly Journal of Economics* 136 (2): 831–86. https://doi.org/10.1093/qje/qjaa042.

Springel, K. 2021. "Network Externality and Subsidy Structure in Two-Sided Markets: Evidence from Electric Vehicle Incentives." *American Economic Journal: Economic Policy* 13 (4): 393–432. https://doi.org/10.1257/pol.20190131.

Urakami, A. 2023. "Are the Barriers to Private Solar/Wind Investment in Viet Nam Mainly Those That Limit Network Capacity Expansion?" *Sustainability* 15 (13): 1–26.

Vona, F., G. Marin, D. Consoli, and D. Popp. 2018. "Environmental Regulation and Green Skills: An Empirical Exploration." *Journal of the Association of Environmental and Resource Economists* 5 (4): 713–53. https://doi.org/10.1086/698859.

Vu, T. 2024. "Southeast Asia's Balancing Act: How Modern Systems Planning Can Help Tackle Demand Forecasting Risks." TransitionZero. https://www.transitionzero.org/insights/southeast-asia-demand-forecasting-risk.

WEF (World Economic Forum). 2022. "Policy Opportunities to Advance Clean Energy Investment in Indonesia." Policy paper, WEF, Geneva. https://www.weforum.org /publications/policy-opportunities-to-advance-clean-energy-investment-in-indonesia/.

World Bank. 2022. *China Country Climate and Development Report*. Washington, DC: World Bank. http://hdl.handle.net/10986/38136.

Zhou, M., F. Chen, and Z. Chen. 2021. "Can CEO Education Promote Environmental Innovation: Evidence from Chinese Enterprises." *Journal of Cleaner Production* 297: 126725. https://doi.org/10.1016/j.jclepro.2021.126725.

Ziegler, M. S., J. M. Mueller, G. D. Pereira, J. Song, M. Ferrara, Y.-M. Chiang, and J. E. Trancik. 2019. "Storage Requirements and Costs of Shaping Renewable Energy toward Grid Decarbonization." *Joule* 3 (9): 2134–53. https://doi.org/10.1016/j.joule.2019.06.012.

How can policy shape the diffusion path of green technology in East Asia and Pacific?

5

The current policy mix

Countries in East Asia and Pacific (EAP) face different policy trade-offs because of variations in their emissions profiles, economic structures, and roles in global decarbonization. China, as the world's largest emitter and a price maker, shapes global energy markets; countries like Indonesia, Malaysia, Thailand, and Viet Nam—although significant emitters—have a more limited global market impact. China and Viet Nam have already seen significant penetration of green technology in energy generation (and in China's case of electric vehicles). Understanding these country-specific differences can help policy makers craft strategies that reduce barriers to the diffusion of green technology.

The policy mix varies substantially within the region and relative to high-income economies (refer to figure 5.1). EAP economies tend to be carbon intensive. Higher scores for the growth in carbon dioxide (CO_2) emissions suggest that economies except Viet Nam are curbing the carbon intensity of their economies.

> The policy mix varies substantially within the region.

> EAP economies are carbon intensive but are investing in renewable energy while largely shying away from taxing carbon emissions or lowering import barriers to green goods.

FIGURE 5.1   Benchmarking EAP performance in carbon emission and policies

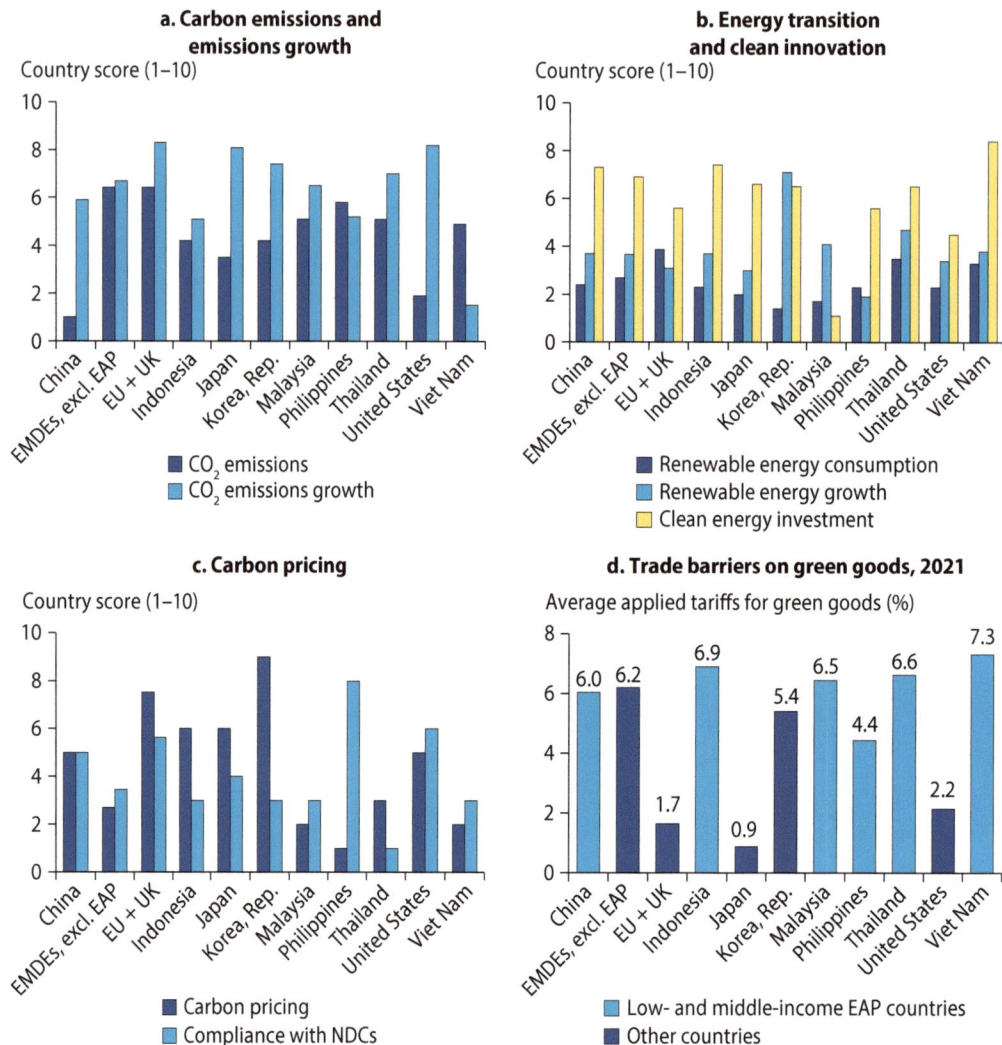

a. Carbon emissions and emissions growth

Country score (1–10)

Legend:
- CO_2 emissions
- CO_2 emissions growth

b. Energy transition and clean innovation

Country score (1–10)

Legend:
- Renewable energy consumption
- Renewable energy growth
- Clean energy investment

c. Carbon pricing

Country score (1–10)

Legend:
- Carbon pricing
- Compliance with NDCs

d. Trade barriers on green goods, 2021

Average applied tariffs for green goods (%)

Values: China 6.0, EMDEs, excl. EAP 6.2, EU + UK 1.7, Indonesia 6.9, Japan 0.9, Korea, Rep. 5.4, Malaysia 6.5, Philippines 4.4, Thailand 6.6, United States 2.2, Viet Nam 7.3

Legend:
- Low- and middle-income EAP countries
- Other countries

Sources: Data from UN Comtrade Database (https://comtradeplus.un.org/) and The Green Future Index (https://www.technologyreview.com/2023/04/05/1070581/the-green-future-index-2023/).

Note: For carbon emissions, energy transition and clean innovation, and carbon pricing, each country is scored from 1 to 10, where 10 corresponds to the best performance. CO_2 emissions refer to total CO_2 emissions in 2019, in millions of tons relative to GDP. CO_2 emissions growth refers to the average annual change in emissions between 2014 and 2019. Renewable energy consumption refers to the percentage of energy from renewable sources out of final energy consumption in 2019. Renewable energy growth is the growth of renewable energy production in gigawatt-hours between 2015 and 2020. Clean energy investment is the amount of investment received and provided for clean energy efforts between 2016 and 2020, as a share of GDP. Compliance with NDCs refers to an evaluation and ranking of policy action to reach stated climate goals in compliance with the Paris Agreement and NDCs. Carbon pricing refers to an assessment and ranking of measures taken by each country to create financial incentives for firms and investors to assign a cost to carbon emissions, through the levying of carbon taxes and the creation of a market for carbon bonds and emissions trading systems. The average applied tariffs on green goods are estimated based on data from Comtrade, where green goods are defined as low-carbon technology goods based on Pigato et al. (2020). CO_2 = carbon dioxide; EAP = East Asia and Pacific; EMDEs = emerging market and developing economies; EU = European Union; excl. = excluding; GDP = gross domestic product; NDCs = nationally determined contributions; UK = United Kingdom.

Renewable energy accounts for a small but growing share of final energy consumption in EAP (refer to figure 5.1, panel b). For example, the use of renewable energy in the Republic of Korea rose from 1 percent of total energy consumption in 2015 to 3 percent in 2021 (US EIA 2023). However, EAP countries have invested significantly in clean innovation. China, Japan, and Korea have registered a disproportionate number of green patents given the size of their economies. China and Viet Nam have invested substantially in clean energy projects in recent years. Like other emerging markets and developing economies (EMDEs), East Asia tends to impose higher tariffs on green goods than high-income economies do (refer to figure 5.1, panel d). The level of ambition toward the net-zero target varies across the region (refer to map 5.1).[1] Cambodia, the Lao People's Democratic Republic, and Viet Nam are committed to achieving net-zero emissions by 2050; China and Indonesia aim to do so by 2060.

The level of ambition toward the net-zero target varies within EAP.

MAP 5.1   **Net-zero targets for participating parties**

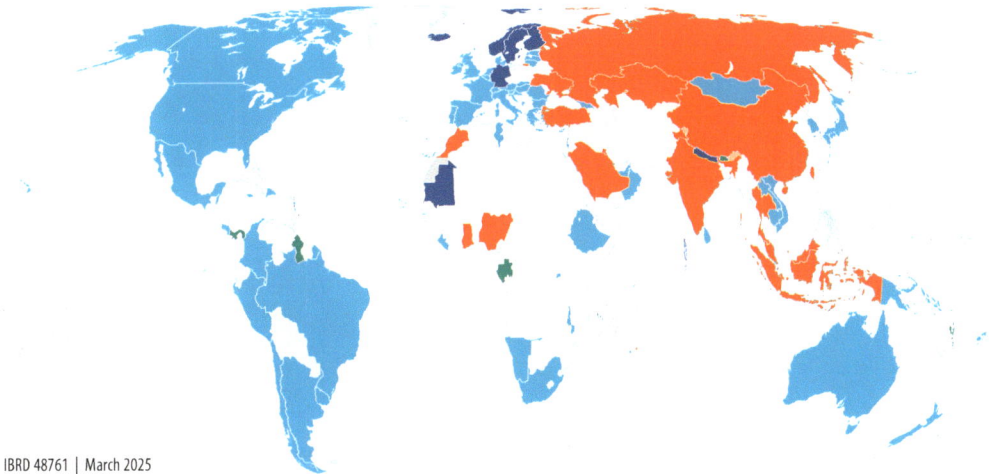

IBRD 48761 | March 2025

Net-zero targets:

- 2050 as target year
- Target year before 2050
- Target year after 2050
- Already achieved and commit to maintain
- No document submitted

Source: Data from Climate Watch (https://www.climatewatchdata.org/net-zero-tracker; https://www.climatewatchdata.org/net-zero-tracker?indicator=nz_year

Political economy constraints have shaped different policy approaches (refer to figures 5.2 and 5.3). The European Union has adopted a comprehensive strategy that integrates carbon pricing mechanisms; capping emissions rather than pricing carbon; and subsidies aimed at fostering the adoption of renewable energy sources, promoting energy efficiency, and transitioning toward a more sustainable economy. By leveraging both regulatory measures and financial incentives, it seeks to drive systemic changes across various sectors, from energy production to transportation and industry. Differences exist within Europe, with Spain focusing on subsidies and Austria and Switzerland focusing more on emissions trading schemes (ETS).

The United States has pursued a different path, emphasizing subsidies and investments in specific green technologies over carbon taxation. This approach reflects a belief in the power of innovation to accelerate the transition to a low-carbon future and the lack of political support toward a more efficient carbon pricing scheme. The 2022 Inflation Reduction Act (IRA) emphasizes the preference for using subsidies instead of taxes for promoting domestic manufacturing, favoring reshoring and friendshoring of inputs critical for the energy transition.

> **Different economies have taken different policy approaches to pricing carbon.**

FIGURE 5.2   Effective carbon rates, various countries

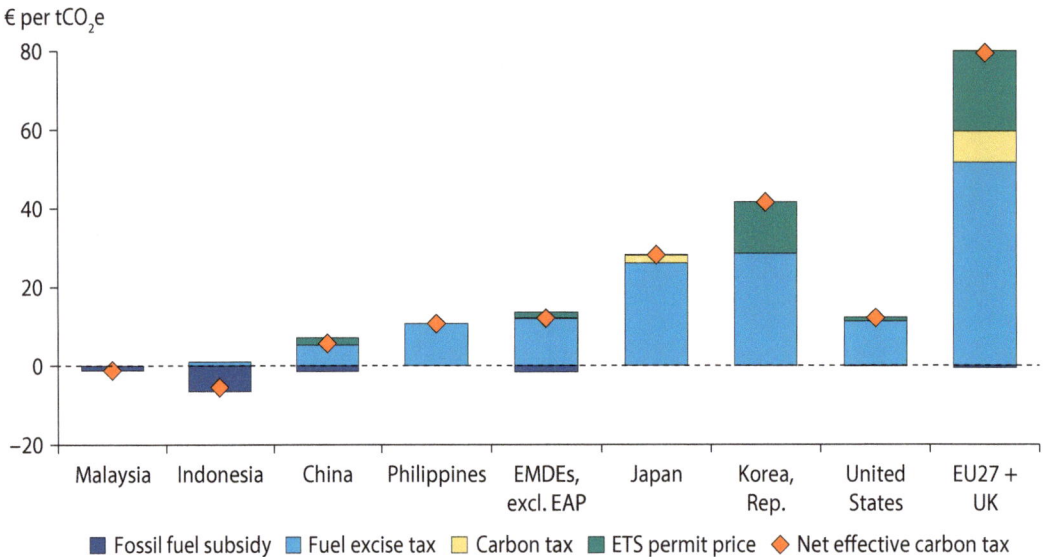

€ per tCO$_2$e

Legend: ■ Fossil fuel subsidy   ■ Fuel excise tax   □ Carbon tax   ■ ETS permit price   ◆ Net effective carbon tax

Sources: Data from Organisation for Economic Co-operation and Development, Data Explorer (https://data-explorer.oecd.org/) and The Green Future Index (https://www.technologyreview.com/2023/04/05/1070581/the-green-future-index-2023/).
Note: Net effective carbon tax corresponds to the effective carbon tax (fuel excise tax + ETS permit price + carbon tax) minus the fossil fuel subsidies. Carbon tax refers to all taxes for which the rate is explicitly linked to the fuel's carbon content, irrespective of whether the resulting carbon price is uniform across fuels and uses. EAP = East Asia and Pacific; EMDEs = emerging market and developing economies; ETS = emissions trading schemes; EU = European Union; excl. = excluding; tCO$_2$e = tons of CO$_2$-equivalent; UK = United Kingdom.

Both green spending and carbon pricing are lower in low- and middle-income EAP than in high-income economies (refer to figure 5.3). The United States and the European Union as well as Korea have introduced significant green spending initiatives through initiatives like the Green New Deal, the Infrastructure Act, and the IRA. The European Union established its ETS in 2005 and has gradually imposed higher prices for CO_2 emissions. In comparison, low- and middle-income EAP countries tend to have lower clean energy spending as a share of GDP

EAP lags high-income countries in carbon pricing and clean energy spending.

FIGURE 5.3   Carbon pricing and clean energy spending, EAP, high-income European countries, and United States, 2020–23

Net effective carbon rate, 2021 (€ per tCO_2e)

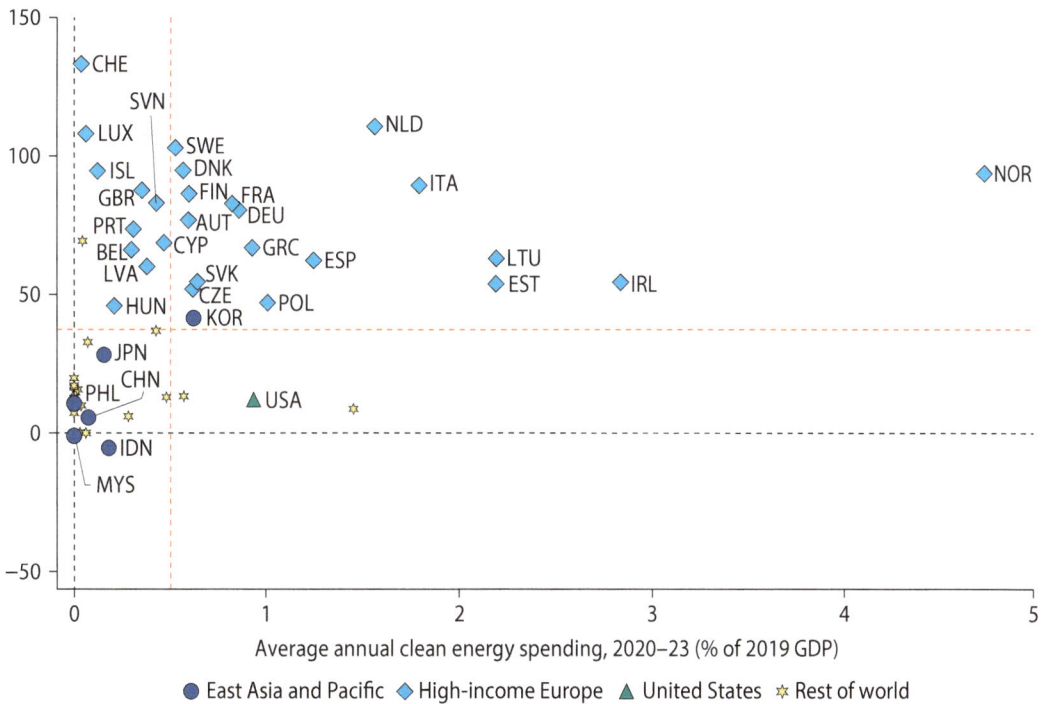

Average annual clean energy spending, 2020–23 (% of 2019 GDP)

● East Asia and Pacific   ◆ High-income Europe   ▲ United States   ☆ Rest of world

Sources: Data from the International Energy Agency on energy spending in 2022–23 (https://www.iea.org/reports/world-energy-investment-2024), the Organisation for Economic Co-operation and Development on effective carbon rates in 2021 (https://data-explorer.oecd.org/), and World Bank, World Development Indicators on 2019 GDP per capita (https://databank.worldbank.org/source/world-development-indicators).

Note: The net effective carbon rate is the net effect of fuel excise taxes, carbon taxes, permit prices, and fuel subsidies (electricity excise taxes and electricity subsidies are not included as they do not distinguish between energy sources and their carbon content). The figures may underestimate overall government support in China because of the shift of support to off-budget instruments. For example, although China recently phased out renewable energy feed-in-tariffs, it continues to support renewable energy in other ways (such as preferential credit terms and access to land) that are not reflected on budget. Dashed orange lines represent cross-country averages. For country codes, refer to https://www.iso.org/obp/ui/#search.

Developing countries in EAP temporarily reversed their fossil fuel subsidy policies in 2022.

FIGURE 5.4   Fossil fuel subsidies in selected EAP countries, 2015–22

Fuel subsidies (% of GDP)

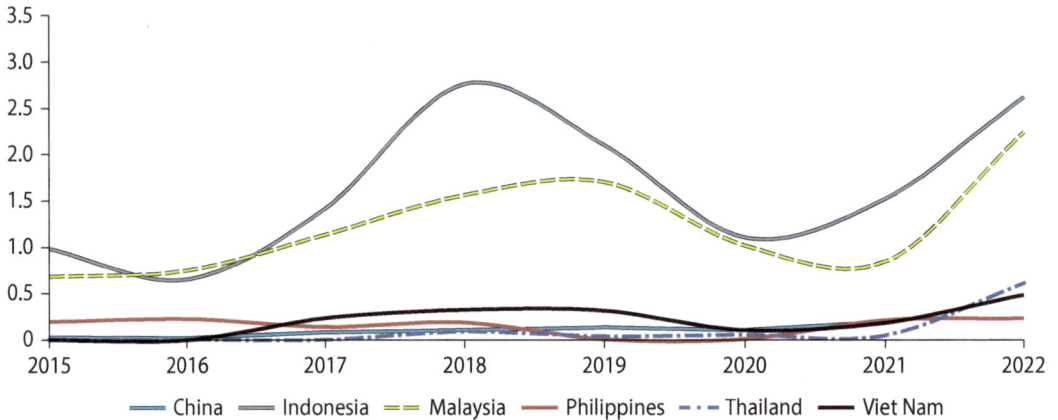

Source: World Bank 2022.
Note: Fuel subsidies declined in some countries in 2023, but 2023 GDP data were not available to compare the trends across the region. EAP = East Asia and Pacific; GDP = gross domestic product.

(refer to figure 5.3). Policy reversals occurred in the early 2020s (refer to figure 5.4), when Indonesia delayed the introduction of a modest carbon tax; Indonesia and Malaysia increased fuel subsidies; Viet Nam reduced environmental taxes on fossil fuels; and China, Indonesia, and Malaysia maintained lower net effective carbon prices and allocated less government spending toward green initiatives than would have been predicted by their income level (refer to figure 5.4).

China stands out within developing EAP, having experimented with ETS. Pilots were launched in selected cities beginning in 2013, and a national ETS became operational in 2021.[2] Their introduction was associated with significant (statistically and economically) increases in the availability of funding for clean-tech start-ups' initial costs (seed funding) and growth (series A) (refer to figure 5.5).[3]

Funding for Chinese clean-tech start-ups increased more rapidly in provinces that implemented an ETS.

FIGURE 5.5   Impact of China's pilot ETS on funding for clean-tech start-ups

Difference in funding amount (IHS transformed)

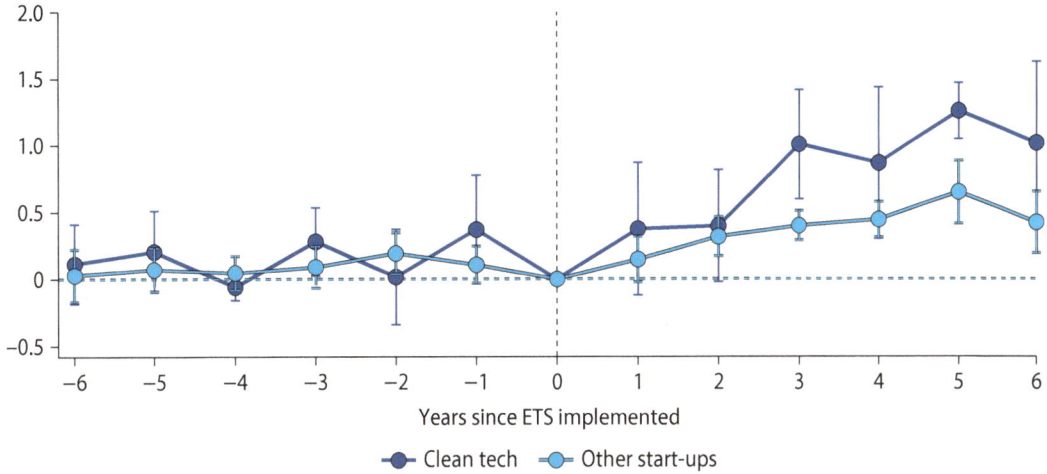

Years since ETS implemented

— Clean tech   — Other start-ups

Source: Data on Chinese start-ups from Crunchbase (https://www.crunchbase.com/).
Note: Results from an event study design

$$Funding_{irt} = \sum_{t} (\delta_t ETS_{rt} + \delta_{rt} ETS_{rt} \times Clean_{irt}) + \gamma\, Age_{irt} + \theta_r + \theta_t + \varepsilon_{irt}$$

where $Funding_{irt}$ indicates the funding amount that firm i in province r at time t receives (at least seed funding or Series A funding). The funding amount uses the inverse hyperbolic sine (IS) transformation to retain zero amount. ETS indicators include an indicator for when the provincial ETS was implemented; $clean_{irt}$ is a dummy whether firm i in province r at time t is a clean-tech start-up. The sample includes funding rounds between 1995 and 2019, limited to active Chinese firms that received at least some funding after 2000. Firms are considered inactive and dropped from the estimation three years after the last funding. Standard errors are clustered at the province level. Whiskers show 95 percent confidence intervals. ETS = emissions trading scheme; IHS = inverse hyperbolic sine.

Policy options and the potential path of green-tech diffusion

The viability of a technology is predictive of the penetration of green technologies like solar PV, which has achieved cost parity with fossil fuels in many parts of the world. Increased viability (decreased cost relative to fossil fuels) is strongly correlated with higher levels of solar penetration across countries (refer to figure 5.6).

Current diffusion patterns also vary widely with policy contexts (fossil fuel subsidies, financial and regulatory support for green tech, the cost of credit) across countries. They have little correlation with the practical potential for solar energy, but they do vary with market and policy environments.[4] Cross-country regression results suggest that conditional on prices, the deployment of solar increases with greater financial and regulatory support and decreases with the level of fossil fuel subsidies and interest rates (refer to figure 5.7). These simple linear results illustrate the potential link between green tech diffusion and market and policy drivers. Nevertheless, actual diffusion patterns often follow a nonlinear path and exhibit strong path dependence, as discussed below.

> Both cost and policy factors predict the pattern of solar diffusion.

FIGURE 5.6   Effect of cost and policy environment on solar PV penetration

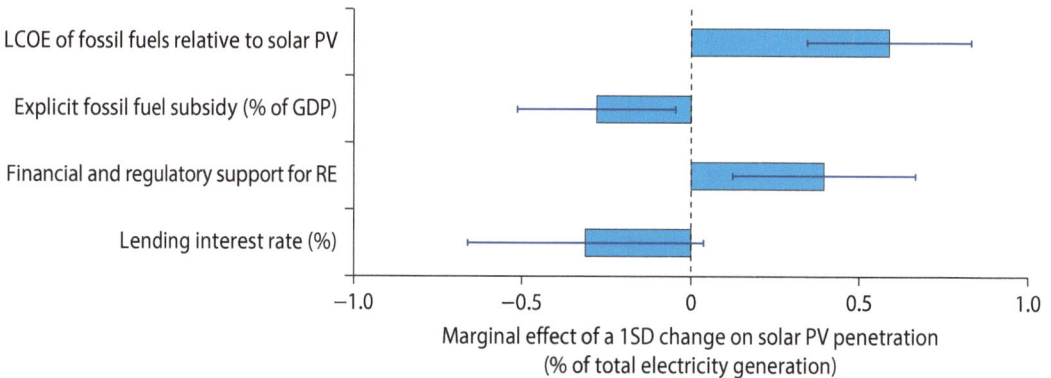

LCOE of fossil fuels relative to solar PV

Explicit fossil fuel subsidy (% of GDP)

Financial and regulatory support for RE

Lending interest rate (%)

Marginal effect of a 1SD change on solar PV penetration
(% of total electricity generation)

Sources: Data on solar penetration from Ember (https://ember-energy.org/data/yearly-electricity-data/); data on solar practical potential from Solargis (https://globalsolaratlas.info/global-pv-potential-study/); data on LCOE from IRENA (https://www.irena.org/Publications/2024/Sep/Renewable-Power-Generation-Costs-in-2023); data on fossil fuel subsidies from IMF (https://www.imf.org/-/media/Files/Topics/energy-subsidies/EXTERNALfuelsubsidiestemplate2023new.ashx); data on support for renewable energy from World Bank, RISE database (https://www.worldbank.org/en/topic/energy/publication/rise---regulatory-indicators-for-sustainable-energy); data on lending interest rates from World Bank, World Development Indicators (https://databank.worldbank.org/source/world-development-indicators).

Note: Figure shows standardized coefficient estimates from a cross-country regression of solar PV penetration between 2015 and 2022. Other controls include GDP per capita, solar practical potential (the power output achievable by a typical configuration of the utility scale PV system), and year fixed effects. Standard errors (the whiskers) are clustered at the country level and indicate 95 percent confidence intervals. GDP = gross domestic product; IMF = International Monetary Fund; IRENA = International Renewable Energy Agency; LCOE = levelized cost of energy; PV = photovoltaic; RE = renewable energy; SD = standard deviation.

Policy instruments to address barriers to green tech diffusion

Technology diffusion often follows a nonlinear path and exhibits strong path dependence (such that early market conditions and policy interventions shape long-term adoption patterns). New technologies evolve through phases of experimentation, early adoption, and eventual mass uptake, with significant barriers often impeding the transition from one stage to the next (Grubb et al. 2021).

Early market conditions and policy interventions shape long-term adoption patterns.

Adjustment costs and path dependence mean that adoption must reach a critical mass for self-sustaining diffusion. As a technology gains more adopters, the process of learning-by-doing reduces costs, accelerating its diffusion. Conversely, if a new technology remains nascent, incumbent technologies maintain their advantage, delaying the transition.

Using a modeling exercise, this section evaluates how policies can address barriers to technology diffusion and affect the potential path of renewable energy penetration in EAP's power sector (Chewpreecha et al. 2025).[5] Barriers such as incumbency advantages,[6] coordination failures, and learning-by-doing complicate the adjustment process. Incumbency advantage can arise from network effects within supply chains, such as the availability of technology-specific skilled labor and the familiarity of investors with established technologies. These factors shape risk perceptions, creating barriers that new technologies cannot immediately overcome, even when the new technology has lower average costs.

So far, this book has emphasized the distinction between viable and nonviable technologies. However, viability is rarely binary; it exists on a spectrum, as different firms and consumers likely face different private costs, because of geographic conditions, resource availability, and market dynamics. The Future Technology Transformation (FTT) model framework (Mercure 2012) allows such cost uncertainties to affect consumer choices, by incorporating probabilistic distributions to capture the effects of differences in costs for the same technology across different projects. When a new technology is cheaper on average but cost is uncertain (more dispersed, as in figure 5.7, panel a), fewer people adopt it than when cost is more certain (less dispersed, as in panel b). In other words, cost uncertainty can slow the adoption of a new technology even as it becomes cheaper on average.

> Adoption of green technology is more gradual when cost is uncertain.

FIGURE 5.7   Quantification of impact of cost distribution and cost certainty on technology adoption

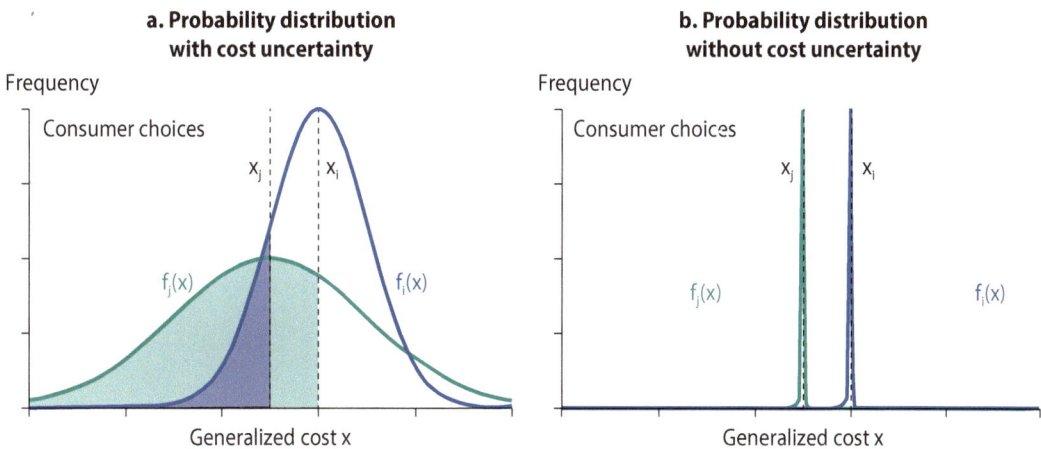

a. Probability distribution with cost uncertainty

b. Probability distribution without cost uncertainty

(continued)

FIGURE 5.7   Quantification of impact of cost distribution and cost certainty on technology adoption
(Continued)

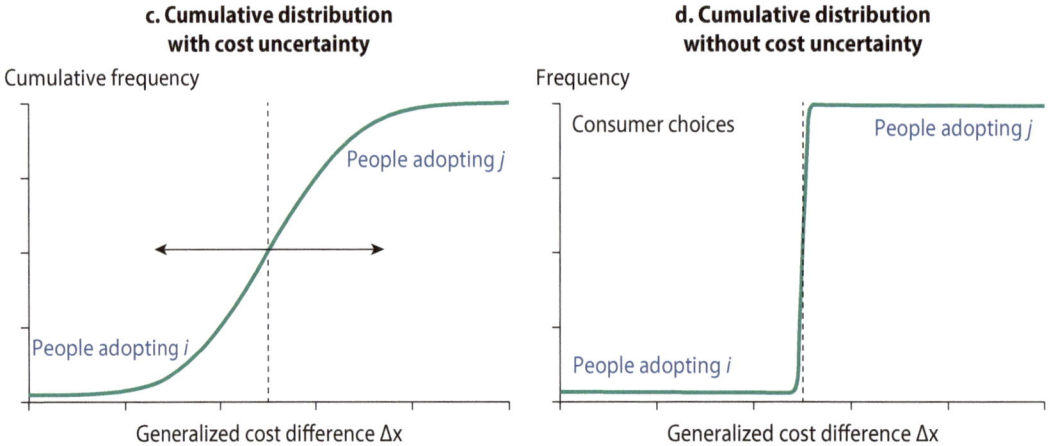

c. Cumulative distribution with cost uncertainty

d. Cumulative distribution without cost uncertainty

Source: Mercure 2012.

Note: Panels a and b show the probability distributions $f_i(x)$ and $f_j(x)$ of the cost values for two technologies i and j based on real recently experienced costs. In panel a, the number of units of technology i that come out at a cost cheaper than the average cost of technology j corresponds to the purple shaded area, a value much smaller than that of the reverse, which is the green area. In panel b, the entire distribution of technology j is to the left of technology i, implying that j is always cheaper than i. Panels c and d show the cumulative probability distribution functions for people adopting i and j.

Table 5.1 reviews the factors that affect technology diffusion and the possible policy responses in the modeling exercise. When multiple frictions are present, adopting a multipronged approach is likely to achieve emissions reductions more cost-effectively than adopting any single measure by itself. The most suitable policy mix will depend on the context, as discussed in the simulation results from Chewpreecha et al. (2025) presented below.

Addressing policy distortions: The case of Indonesia

In Indonesia, the playing field is tilted in favor of coal. Infrastructure and long-term purchasing contracts that fix prices and guarantee the quantity of coal-generated electricity create significant barriers to the transition toward clean energy. The incumbency advantage is reinforced by coal pricing subsidies that artificially lower the cost of coal-fired power and impose a significant burden on public finance. Shortening the lifetime of a coal power plant (a proxy for lifting price guarantees) coupled with removing coal subsidies can catalyze the adoption of cleaner energy and accelerate emission reductions.

TABLE 5.1   Factors and policy implications affecting diffusion of green technology in the FTT model framework

Factor	Explanation	Example (coal versus solar)	Possible policy response
Incumbency advantage	Incumbent firms benefit from existing infrastructure and labor, slowing adoption of new technology.	Coal's dominant market share slows solar growth even when solar costs less than coal.	• Coal phaseout programs • Incentives for solar supply chains and workforce • Kick-start of solar program
Technology replacement rate	The speed of the transition depends on the speed with which existing fossil fuel power plants can retire and the construction time for new renewable energy facilities.	Solar farms take two years to build; coal plants last 40 or more years.	• Faster permitting for solar • Coal phaseout program
Cost competitiveness	Cost variability within each technology type limits adoption of new technology even if new technology has lower average costs.	Solar may be cheaper overall but less competitive in cloudy regions.	• Carbon pricing • Subsidies for solar • Policy to reduce variability in costs of solar
Learning-by-doing	Capital and operations and maintenance (O&M) costs decline because of learning-by-doing, as reflected in installed capacity, in line with the presence of learning curves (refer to chapter 2).	Solar capital costs drop by 0.25 percent for every 1 percent increase in global installed capacity; solar O&M costs drop by 0.25 percent for every 1 percent increase in domestic installed capacity.	• Support for scaling up solar deployment • International cooperation to increase global solar capacity • Removal of tariffs on solar technology imports

Source: Chewpreecha et al. 2025.
Note: FTT = Future Technology Transformation.

Figure 5.8 shows the diffusion of solar and the associated reduction in CO_2 emissions attributable to shortening the lifetime of coal plants (normally about 40 years). Reductions of 1 or 2 years have only a marginal impact, but reduction by 10 years could cut the share of coal-generated electricity and emissions by about 10 percent.

Reducing the lifespan of coal power plants in Indonesia by 10 years could reduce the share of coal-generated electricity and emissions by about 10 percent.

FIGURE 5.8   **Impact of reduction in the lifespan of coal power plants on solar share and CO_2 reductions, Indonesia, 2050**

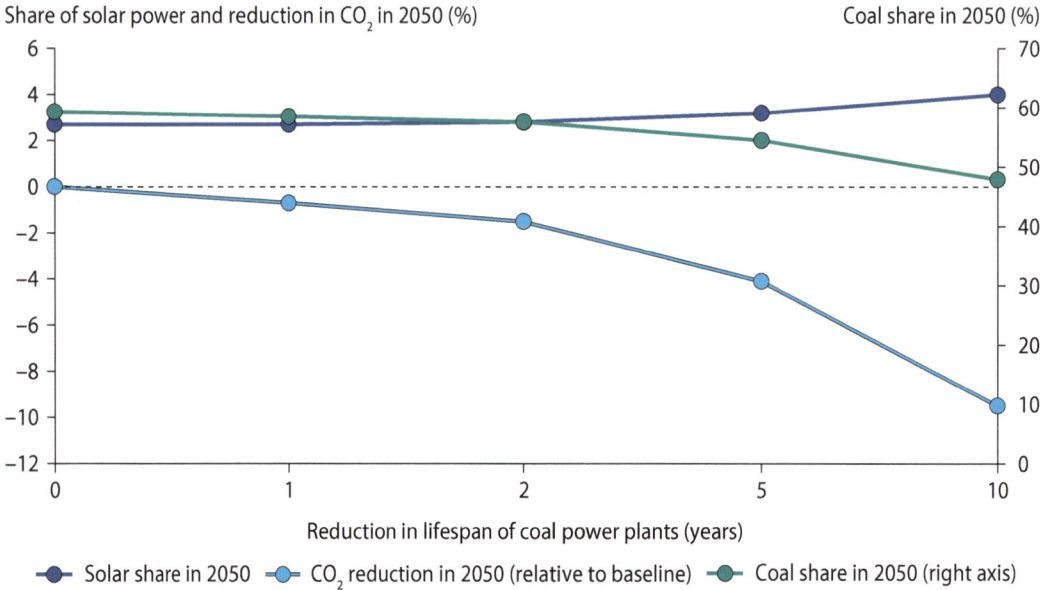

Source: Chewpreecha et al. 2025.
Note: CO_2 = carbon dioxide.

Setting effective carbon taxes at different stages of solar diffusion: The case of Thailand

Thailand's power sector is dominated by gas (and to a significantly smaller extent coal); solar accounts for less than 3 percent of electricity generation. The dominance of gas creates significant inertia in the system.

The extent to which a carbon tax can cut emissions and promote solar diffusion depends on the current share of solar in the energy mix. Simulation results suggest that introducing the same carbon tax may raise the share of solar power in the energy mix by 16 to 67 percent, depending on whether solar shares remain at the 2023 level (2.8 percent) or rise to 25 percent (refer to figure 5.9). Introducing carbon taxes after solar deployment reaches about 15 percent (about the level of China and Viet Nam) can deliver larger emission reductions at every level of carbon tax, accelerating the diffusion of clean energy.

> **A carbon tax is more effective at promoting solar diffusion at higher levels of solar share in the energy mix.**

FIGURE 5.9   Growth of solar share under two policy assumptions, Thailand, 2023–50

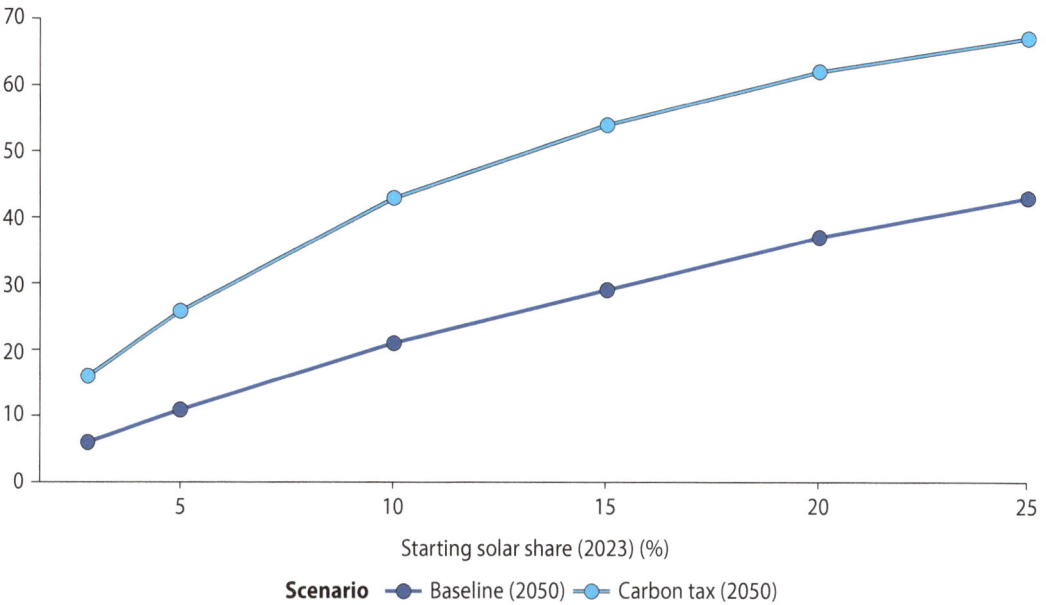

Solar share (2050) (%)

Source: Chewpreecha et al. 2025.

Understanding the implications of different emission reduction policies: The case of Viet Nam

Viet Nam's power sector relies heavily on coal and hydropower, but new renewable energy sources, particularly solar, have grown rapidly in recent years, increasing from less than 1 percent of total power generation in 2018 to 11.5 percent in 2022.[7] This momentum is promising, but achieving net-zero emissions by 2050 will require much more rapid adoption of green energy.

Policy makers can use a range of policy instruments to reduce emissions. Mandating a one-time 3.3 percent increase such that solar's share of power generation reaches 15 percent in 2025 could achieve a cumulative reduction of 292 metric tons of CO_2 ($MtCO_2$) emissions reduction between 2025 and 2050. The same cumulative reduction target can be reached in the following ways:

• Providing subsidies covering 88 percent of the capital costs of solar projects in 2024–50
• Imposing a carbon tax starting at US$10.50 per ton in 2025 and rising to US$100 per ton by 2050
• Reducing the lifetime of coal plants by 7 years (from 40 to 33 years).

Figure 5.10 shows the emission-reduction paths associated with each of these policy options. Emissions drop early with a solar share mandate; other options deliver more substantial emission reductions later on. These differences reflect the mechanisms underlying each policy. A solar mandate can help coordinate the rapid development required of supporting infrastructure, providing an immediate boost to solar deployment. A carbon tax that increases over time has only a limited effect initially, but its sustained price signal encourages a structural transition from coal to solar, resulting in more significant emissions savings in later years.

Each policy option comes with distinct economic trade-offs:

- A carbon tax creates both consumption and production deadweight losses but benefits the government through tax revenue.
- Both solar subsidies and a solar share mandate create a production deadweight loss by pushing green production beyond optimal levels, but they differ in who bears the cost burden: Subsidies require government funding, whereas a mandate shifts costs to private solar producers.

> **Different policy tools have distinct effects on the path of emissions reductions.**

FIGURE 5.10   Emissions reductions in Viet Nam under four policy assumptions, 2024–50

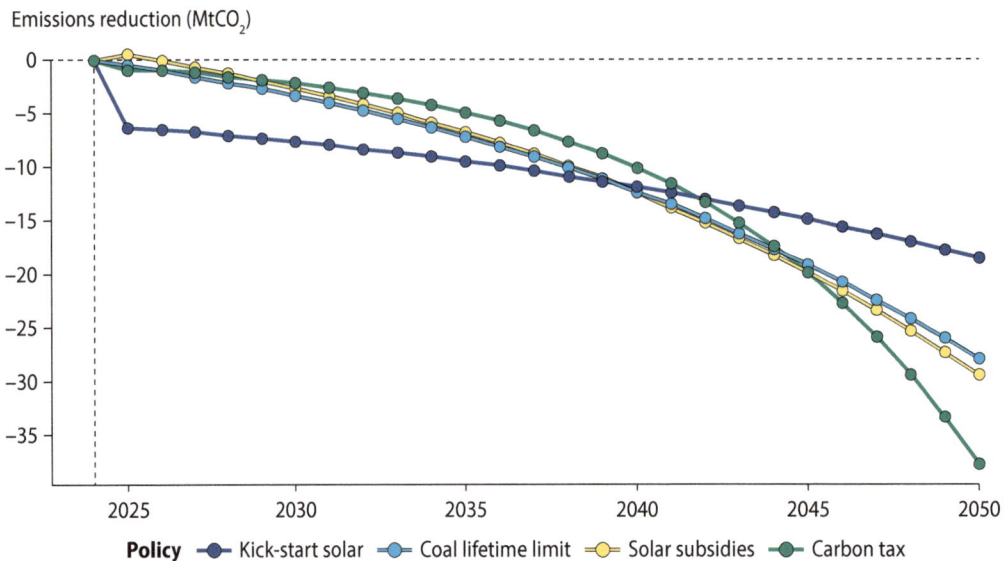

Emissions reduction (MtCO$_2$)

Policy —•— Kick-start solar   —•— Coal lifetime limit   —○— Solar subsidies   —•— Carbon tax

Source: Chewpreecha et al. 2025.

Note: MtCO$_2$ = megatonnes carbon dioxide.

- A coal lifetime limit, like a carbon tax, imposes both consumption and production deadweight losses by forcing coal generators to absorb higher fixed costs over a shorter period. However, a lifetime limit has a higher economic cost, because it does not generate government revenue like a carbon tax does.

Driving global learning-by-doing: The case of China

Given the scale of China's energy system, its policy choices have significant impacts on global markets, as simulations show. By 2045, a policy mix including a carbon tax, energy-efficiency regulations, subsidies for renewable energy, and the early phaseout of coal-fired power plants to achieve China's twin goals of peaking emissions by 2030 and achieving carbon neutrality by 2060 should reduce the levelized cost of solar outside China by 3.7 percent compared with the baseline. Solar power generation increases by almost 10 percent, because of a combination of the lower costs of and higher demand for electrification of transport and household heating, a result of technology spillovers from China. Emissions outside of China could decline by more than 3 percent because of changes in the energy mix (refer to figure 5.11).

Learning-by-doing spillovers from China have a large effect on the rest of the world.

FIGURE 5.11   Global spillover benefits from China's climate actions, 2025–60

Change from baseline (%)

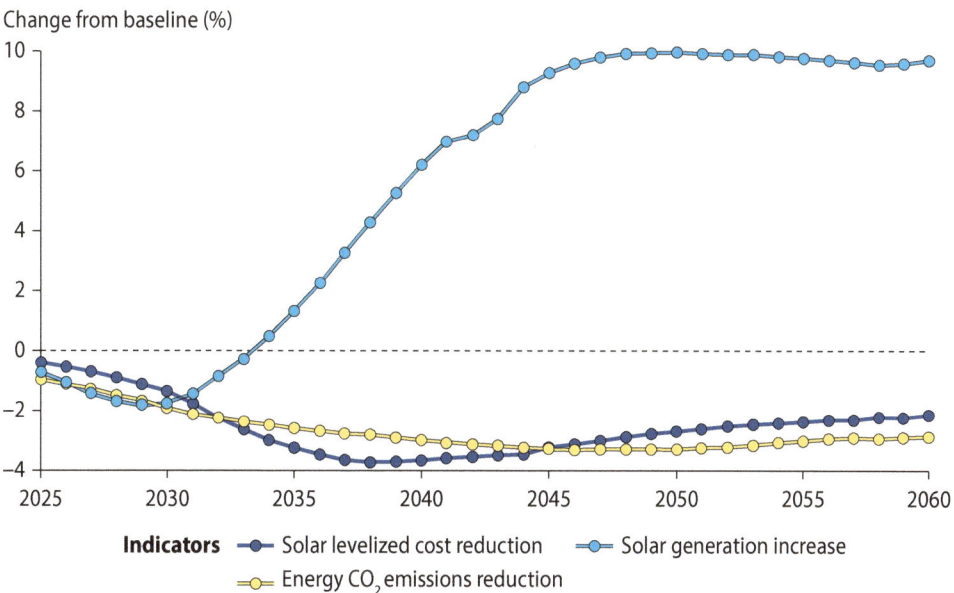

Indicators ── Solar levelized cost reduction   ── Solar generation increase
── Energy CO_2 emissions reduction

Source: Chewpreecha et al. 2025.
Note: Figure excludes China. CO_2 = carbon dioxide.

Conclusion

To sum up, eliminating distortionary policies, such as fossil fuel subsidies, would deliver both economic and environmental benefits. Where existing power purchase agreements offer long-term assured prices for fossil fuel–generated power, as in Indonesia, it may help to limit the life of power plants.

Win-wins could also be harvested by addressing domestic market failures, such as those arising from coordination failures and dynamic economies of scale, which limit investment in green infrastructure. Given the high fixed costs associated with building and adopting new technologies, as well as the need for synchronized action across interdependent areas (infrastructure, skills), a kick-start through centrally coordinated quantitative targets may be necessary in countries with low shares of renewables, such as Malaysia, the Philippines, and Thailand. Prior policy action to remedy policy distortions (such as long-term power purchase agreements) and coordination failures (such as kick-starts) is likely to increase the efficacy of these fiscal instruments.

Political challenges affect the feasibility of different policy options. Policies that impose direct costs on businesses or consumers (such as carbon taxes or early coal retirements) may face stronger opposition from industry stakeholders. Subsidy-driven policies may be more politically palatable, but they require fiscal resources; the raising or diverting of resources may provoke opposition from those who bear the cost. Given the path-dependent nature of technology diffusion and political opposition from specific groups, a combination of policies may provide the most effective approach to decarbonization.

Notes

1. Net-zero greenhouse gas emissions (or greenhouse gas neutrality) occurs if anthropogenic removals balance anthropogenic greenhouse gas emissions to the atmosphere over a specific period (IPCC 2018).
2. See the appendix for an overview of carbon pricing schemes in the region.
3. Series A funding refers to funding rounds for early-stage companies. On average, it raises US$1 million–US$15 million.
4. "Practical potential" refers to the power output achievable by a typical configuration of a utility-scale PV system.
5. The model incorporates the diffusion characteristics identified by Mercure (2012)—including path dependency, learning-by-doing, time constraints for new and old technologies, and cost uncertainties—by allowing for heterogeneity among agents in terms of the costs associated with both existing and new technologies. This report uses two variations of the Future Technology Transformation (FTT) model: (1) the FTT-FLEX model (which abstracts from global spillovers) for smaller countries and (2) the full FTT (which accounts for a country's adoption effects on global learning-by-doing and is applicable to China) for global coverage.

6. A technology with plenty of installed capacity in the domestic market will have several advantages over an incipient technology, independent of costs. Having seen a technology applied elsewhere, investors will have greater confidence in it, reducing uncertainty around projects and perception of risks. This hysteresis in the evolution of costs and the diffusion of technologies helps explain why older, well-established technologies may persist even when new technologies have lower costs.

7. Based on data from Ember (https://ember-energy.org/data/yearly-electricity-data/).

References

Chewpreecha, U., A. Mattoo, H. Pollitt, and Thu Trang Tran. 2025 "Evidence from East Asia on Pricing and Quantitative Low Carbon Policy Instruments." Unpublished paper, World Bank, Washington, DC.

Grubb, M., P. Drummond, A. Poncia, W. McDowall, D. Popp, S. Samadi, et al. 2021. "Induced Innovation in Energy Technologies and Systems: A Review of Evidence and Potential Implications for CO_2 Mitigation." *Environmental Research Letters* 16 (4): 043007. https://doi.org/10.1088/1748-9326/abde07.

IPCC (Intergovernmental Panel on Climate Change). 2018. *Global Warming of 1.5°C: IPCC Special Report on Impacts of Global Warming of 1.5°C above Pre-industrial Levels in Context of Strengthening Response to Climate Change, Sustainable Development, and Efforts to Eradicate Poverty*. Cambridge, UK: Cambridge University Press. https://doi.org/10.1017/9781009157940.

Mercure, J. F. 2012. "FTT: Power: A Global Model of the Power Sector with Induced Technological Change and Natural Resource Depletion." *Energy Policy* 48: 799–811.

Pigato, M., S. J. Black, D. Dussaux, Z. Mao, M. McKenna, R. Rafaty, and S. Touboul. 2020. *Technology Transfer and Innovation for Low-Carbon Development*. International Development in Focus. Washington, DC: World Bank. http://hdl.handle.net/10986/33474.

US EIA (US Energy Information Administration). 2023. "South Korea." Washington, DC. https://www.eia.gov/international/analysis/country/KOR.

World Bank. 2022. "Reforms for Recovery." World Bank East Asia and Pacific Economic Update. World Bank, Washington, DC. doi: https://doi.org/10.1596/978-1-4648-1921-6.

Considerations for policy | 6

Next steps

Current trade frictions and the resulting restrictions on access to markets and technology in East Asia and Pacific (EAP) suggest that the region and the rest of the world cannot rely only on the green fruits of industrial rivalry. Measures to encourage the domestic diffusion of cleaner technologies in EAP will improve the global environment, by reducing export surpluses, and may help diffuse the international tensions that are provoking restrictions on trade and technology flows.

EAP countries need to determine what to do, when to do it, and whether to act alone or in coordination with other countries. This chapter examines these choices in light of the analysis in this report.

The policy balance for discovery and diffusion

Supporting the discovery and adoption of clean technologies requires multiple policy instruments to tackle different types of market failures. The existence of knowledge spillovers motivates subsidies for research and development (R&D) on clean technologies. Addressing negative environmental externalities calls for the introduction of carbon pricing mechanisms. Acemoglu et al. (2016) provide a theoretical framework in which the optimal policy mix incorporates both subsidies and carbon pricing mechanisms tailored to address these two types of externalities.

> Effective policy requires multiple instruments and sequencing that accounts for technologies' viability.

The timing of policy matters. Given that technological advances in one sector make future advances in that sector more productive or more profitable, front-loading R&D subsidies within cleaner sectors during the nascent stages accelerates the transition toward an improved equilibrium. As the viability of clean technologies improves, taxes are gradually increased to encourage diffusion on the optimal path. Such proactive measures are deemed essential for steering the trajectory of technological innovation toward environmentally sustainable pathways.

This book emphasizes the role of direct assistance in promoting discovery and the role of taxes in promoting diffusion, noting that both green subsidies and carbon taxes have been effective in redirecting innovation toward green technologies. The history of the solar industry demonstrates how different policy tools have been used to increase the viability and adoption of technology (refer to special focus 2.1, in chapter 2). China's solar production and innovation subsidies increased both the number of solar manufacturing firms as well as their production scale, innovation, and productivity (Banares-Sanchez et al. 2024). On the tax dimension, Aghion et al. (2016) show how the auto industry increases clean innovation because of increases in tax-inclusive fuel prices. Further, they argue that evidence of path dependency in innovation, where future innovations build on the cumulative knowledge of the industry as well as the firm's own innovation history, means that carbon taxes are needed to overcome the lock-in of dirty technologies. Similarly, the European Union's carbon emission trading scheme (ETS) and the pilot carbon ETS in China have stimulated the patenting and R&D of new low-carbon technologies (Calel 2020; Ren et al. 2022). The appropriate type of policy interventions may also be linked to the level of maturity of technologies (Johnstone, Haščič, and Popp 2010).

Most emerging market and developing economies (EMDEs), with the notable exception of China, rely on technologies that have been developed in other countries. The focus of policy has therefore been more on the optimal policy mix to promote diffusion—that is, legs 1, 2, and 3 of the policy framework shown in figure 1.5, in chapter 1. The distinction between economically viable and nonviable technologies is not always clear-cut, especially in phases when new technologies are still emerging; technology costs can decline through learning-by-doing; technology replacement faces both construction delays and the long-life of existing investments; and complementary inputs may be in short supply. In these circumstances, firms face impediments arising from inadequate information, imperfect capital markets, and coordination failures involving infrastructure and skills development, as well as policy biases in favor of incumbent technologies. Chapter 5 demonstrated that the optimal policy mix to encourage diffusion is, therefore, likely to involve a combination of interventions to address these different forms of market and policy imperfections.

The political economy of technology policies

Political support for green technology policies depends on the potential impact on different interest groups. Where policies encourage the adoption of economically viable technologies by eliminating policy distortions (such as fuel subsidies) or addressing market failures (such as imperfect information), the net economic benefit is positive. In these cases, it is possible in principle to compensate the losers, so that the policy can be Pareto improving, but transfers may be hard to effect in practice. Policies to encourage the adoption of technologies that are not yet viable impose a net economic cost and are likely to face greater political opposition unless there is sufficient appreciation of the climate benefits or the co-benefits in terms of reduced pollution. Table 6.1 shows how the burden of the policy interventions discussed in chapter 5 are distributed across different groups.

Support for green tech policy hinges on balancing economic impacts across stakeholders.

Careful sequencing of policies may help overcome political economy barriers to the green transition. Carbon pricing, green mandates, and efficiency standards may need to be phased in and complemented with support to soften opposition from the owners of potentially stranded assets (Rozenberg, Vogt-Schilb, and Hallegatte 2020). Survey evidence from 20 countries confirms that support for subsidies to low-carbon technologies is greater than support for carbon pricing (Dechezleprêtre et al., forthcoming).

TABLE 6.1   Economic burden of power sector policies across stakeholders

Policy	Brown producers	Green producers	Consumers	Government
Carbon tax	Negative (higher costs, reduced competitiveness)	Positive (higher competitiveness because of coal cost increase)	Negative (higher electricity price)	Transfers from producers to government via tax revenues
Solar subsidies	Negative (reduced competitiveness)	Positive (lower capital costs, increased deployment)	Positive (if subsidies are passed on to final electricity price)	Transfers from government to green producers through subsidies
Green kick-start	Negative (reduced competitiveness)	Negative if implemented only because mandated by government	May not affect consumers if green technology has a higher levelized cost of electricity	Transfers from government to green producers if funded publicly
Limit on coal lifetime	Negative (stranded assets, lost revenues)	Positive (opportunities to replace coal generation)	Negative (if additional costs are passed on to consumers)	No transfers (unless government chooses to compensate brown producers)

Source: Chewpreecha et al. 2025.

Politically salient objectives, such as "green jobs," may be a way to promote the green transition (Rodrik 2014). But politicians may pay (politically) for implementing inefficient programs. De Groote, Gautier, and Verboven (2024) study the political reaction to a generous solar-panel subsidization program. Belgian voters punished incumbent parties upon realizing that the financing costs would be high, fall largely on nonbeneficiary taxpayers, and benefit foreign solar panel producers. This example suggests that green industrial policies, which seek to boost local production of green goods rather than local consumption, may be easier to sell than other policies.

Domestic adoption amid global competition and cooperation

EAP countries may be tempted to wait for cheaper technologies to emerge through the efforts of the rest of the world rather than adopt still-expensive technologies today. Past policies such as solar feed-in-tariffs in Germany increased global demand for solar power by 78 percent between 2010 and 2015, with over half of that increase from lower costs from innovation induced by the subsidies (Gerarden 2023). Heavy spending by China, the United States, and the European Union may have similar spillover effects.[1]

> **The temptation to wait for cheaper technologies must be weighed against the benefits of energy independence and domestic learning-by-doing.**

However, the spillover effects of other economies' green spending are not automatic. Market structure plays a crucial role in determining how declines in the cost of green technologies translate into affordability for developing countries. Competition dynamics among international firms, as well as the level of competition within EMDEs, affect the distribution of benefits and costs across regions. Spillover effects also depend on institutional factors, including intellectual property rights regimes and technology transfer policies. The current subsidy wars have increased access to low-priced green goods, benefiting EMDE consumers of these products, although they have not yet ensured access to green technologies, which would benefit producers of these products.

The case for a swifter transition rests, first, on the promise of energy independence and diminished exposure to the volatility of global energy markets. Second, an early transition can be more cost-effective because of the existence of learning curves within countries, as discussed in chapter 2 and by evidence of dynamic spillovers and path dependency (Aghion et al. 2016). The magnitude of between-firm innovation spillovers may be larger for green technologies than for their dirty counterparts (Verhoeven and Martin 2024). However, the rate at which the cost of adoption falls is not homogeneous across countries. For example, the productivity of wind turbines in China was well below that of the United States, because of multiple factors, including delays in grid connection, curtailment of energy because of grid management, and suboptimal turbine selection and wind farm design (Hayashi, Huenteler, and Lewis 2018; Huenteler et al. 2018).

A coordinated global effort to cut emissions could lead to an earlier transition (refer to box 6.1). Such collective action would be in the interests of EAP countries, because they are among the most exposed to the consequences of climate change.

Box 6.1.   What is the national and globally optimal amount of emissions?

The analysis in this report helps distinguish between the set of policy interventions a country would (unilaterally) benefit from and the set of pro-climate actions that it would benefit from as part of a larger global effort. It helps identify where international cooperation or support are needed to reduce a country's emissions and when (unilateral) national action is sufficient.

Consider the following stylized framework. Figure B6.1.1 shows the expected present discounted value of changes in welfare resulting from an additional unit of emissions reduction. The optimal level of reduction corresponds to the peak of the curves (the point at which the first derivative of the welfare function is equal to zero), as explained below.

What is in a country's national economic interest?

The national income curve depicted in figure B6.1.1 captures the purely economic impact of emissions reductions, conditional on the current state of technology. The upward-sloping segment of the curve reflects the reduction in emissions achieved by the removal of policy and market distortions (when technologies are viable, as depicted in the left half of the figure). Cutting emissions to O_1^* can be accomplished by removing fossil fuel subsidies, removing trade restrictions, and/or addressing imperfections in the credit market. Elimination of deadweight losses related to these distortions implies a potential economic and environmental win-win. Movements along the upward-sloping segment can arise from any measures that increase energy efficiency as well as from the productivity gains that arise from less pollution, which could be a co-benefit of emissions reduction (Graff Zivin and Neidell 2012). In each of these cases, a country reaps both environmental and economic benefits and therefore does not require external support. As more green technologies become economically viable, one would expect O_1^* to shift to the right.

(continued)

Box 6.1.   What is the national and globally optimal amount of emissions? *(Continued)*

> Emissions reductions depend on whether a country is optimizing for the national or the global welfare.

FIGURE B6.1.1   Expected present discounted value of changes in welfare resulting from an additional unit of emissions reduction

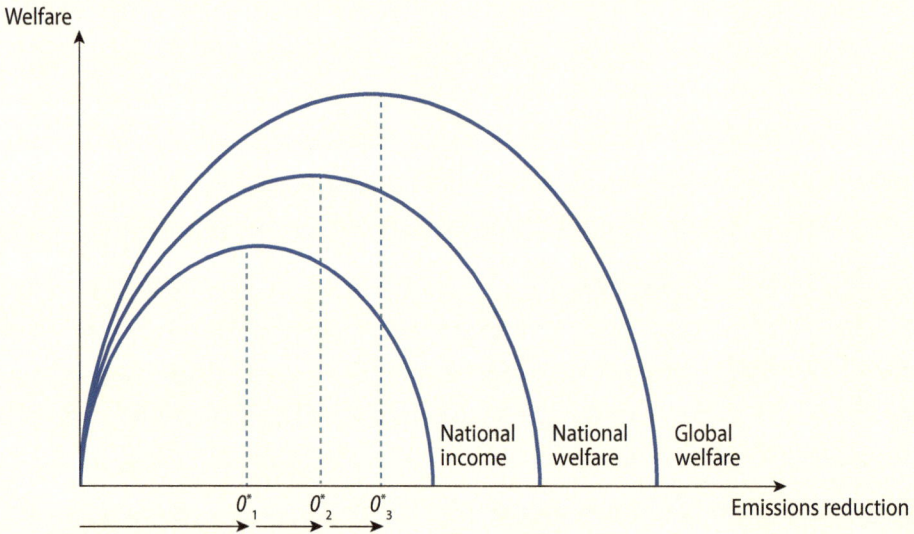

Source: Original figure for this publication.
Note: The solid lines are welfare curves from the reduction in emissions. O^* captures the optimal level of emissions reduction under the different scenarios.

Lack of action to achieve O_1^* can be explained by two types of distributional effects that make the political economy of reform difficult. The first is concerns that higher energy costs will disproportionately affect the poor. In principle, this concern can be addressed by strengthening instruments to compensate them by drawing on the resources freed up by the removal of distortions/deadweight losses. Indonesia's reduction in fossil fuel subsidies in 2012 was accompanied by an expansion in social protection and increased spending on health and education.

The second effect is resistance to emissions cuts coming from vested interests in the fossil fuel sectors. Devising measures to legitimately compensate the rich and powerful is politically more difficult. The Asian Development Bank proposed buying out investors in coal in Indonesia who benefited from relatively generous power purchase agreements (ADB 2023).

(continued)

Box 6.1.   What is the national and globally optimal amount of emissions? *(Continued)*

What is in a country's national interest more broadly?

The national welfare curve captures not just changes in national income but also changes in national welfare that come from a country's own emissions reductions. The wedge between the national income curve and the national welfare curve for any given unit of emissions reduction represents the aggregate noneconomic benefits of decarbonization. Examples of such benefits include improvement in global climate for the country as well as lower domestic pollution-related harm, especially to children and older people (Currie and Walker 2011; Neidell 2004). Moving from O_1^* to O_2^* can yield additional national welfare benefits but involves a decline in national income, because measures required to reduce emissions, such as carbon taxes or green subsidies, create a purely economic deadweight losses. As the move to O_2^* is welfare enhancing, a country should pursue it unilaterally, although a poor country may still require external assistance to deal with the economic costs of transition.

What is in the global interest?

The global welfare curve captures the impact of a country's emissions cuts on global welfare. Moving from O_2^* to O_3^* requires greater use of economically costly instruments (carbon taxes or green subsidies). Using these instruments may not be in the country's own interest but would yield benefits for the world. This additional emissions reduction therefore requires international cooperation. Nationally Determined Contributions under the Paris Agreement are expected to fall well short of O_3^*.

The enhanced viability of green technologies would limit the need for costly economic instruments to encourage diffusion. Promoting green technologies would narrow the wedge between the national income and global welfare curves and shrink the distance between O_1^* and O_3^*. But enhancing viability is costly, because it requires support for research and development (R&D) or output increases that spur learning-by-doing (although there is evidence that shifting more public resources to clean technology R&D does not imply lower economic returns [Martin and Verhoeven 2022]).

It is conceivable that one day countries will collaborate in implementing a package of support for the development of technologies and taxes to encourage their diffusion. Today, however, support is coming not from a cooperative climate motive but from rivalrous industrial policy goals, and there is still limited appetite to implement carbon taxes.

Three types of policy actions for EAP countries

The analysis in this book suggests three types of policy actions for EAP countries. They are listed here in order of priority:

- Eliminating distortionary policies—including fossil fuel subsidies, inefficient dispatch policies, and trade and investment barriers—would deliver both economic and environmental benefits. Where power purchase agreements offer long-term assured prices for fossil fuel–generated power, it may be necessary to limit the life of power plants. Complementary measures—such as providing assistance for low-income beneficiaries of fuel subsidies and retraining workers displaced from fossil fuel industries—would enhance the economic benefits and reduce the political difficulty of reforms.
- Win-wins could be harvested by addressing domestic market failures, such as those arising from imperfections in information, which limit credit to green innovations, and imperfections in coordination, which limit investment in green infrastructure. Given the high fixed costs associated with building and adopting new technologies, as well as the need for synchronized action across interdependent areas (infrastructure, skills), a kick-start through centrally coordinated quantitative targets may help boost diffusion. For small, low-income countries, remedying such market imperfections unilaterally would be difficult, because of lack of capacity.
- Going further toward inducing the adoption of nonviable technologies—through carbon taxes or green subsidies—involves incurring an economic cost to secure an environmental benefit. Prior policy action to remedy policy distortions and market failures is likely to increase the efficacy of these fiscal instruments. How far EAP countries are willing to go in deploying them depends on the international commitments they have already made as well as the benefits they receive, through emissions cuts, assistance, and technology transfers by the rest of the world.

The first two types of action unambiguously increase national welfare and can be undertaken unilaterally as soon as the necessary complementary reforms and support are in place. Whether the third improves national welfare depends on what the rest of the world does and therefore can be undertaken at a pace and on a scale determined by past international commitments and future international cooperation. In general, deeper reform of the region's climate, trade, industrial, and innovation policies is likely to foster mutually beneficial international cooperation in each of these areas.

Note

1. Larsen and others (2023) project that the technology and innovation "spillover" effects from the Inflation Reduction Act (IRA) could generate larger emissions savings outside the United States, with 2.4–2.9 tons of carbon dioxide reductions abroad for every ton saved domestically by the end of the century. Policy interventions in China, including both subsidies and regulatory measures, may have significant impact on global learning-by-doing and reductions in emissions (see chapter 5).

References

Acemoglu, D., U. Akcigit, D. Hanley, and W. Kerr. 2016. "Transition to Clean Technology." *Journal of Political Economy* 124 (1): 52–104. https://doi.org/10.1086/684511.

ADB (Asian Development Bank). 2023. "New Agreement Aims to Retire Indonesia 660-MW Coal Plant Almost 7 Years Early." Press release, December 3. Manila. https://www.adb.org /news/new-agreement-aims-retire-indonesia-660-mw-coal-plant-almost-7-years-early.

Aghion, P., A. Dechezleprêtre, D. Hémous, R. Martin, and J. Van Reenen. 2016. "Carbon Taxes, Path Dependency, and Directed Technical Change: Evidence from the Auto Industry." *Journal of Political Economy* 124 (1): 1–51. https://doi.org/10.1086/684581.

Banares-Sanchez, I., R. Burgess, D. Laszlo, P. Simpson, J. V. Reenen, and Y. Wang. 2024. "Chinese Innovation, Green Industrial Policy and the Rise of Solar Energy." https:// economics.unibocconi.eu/sites/default/files/files/media/attachments/ray_of_hope___paper %288%2920240412112838.pdf.

Calel, R. 2020. "Adopt or Innovate: Understanding Technological Responses to Cap-and-Trade." *American Economic Journal: Economic Policy* 12 (3): 170–201. https://doi.org/10.1257/pol.20180135.

Chewpreecha, U., A. Mattoo, H. Pollitt, and T. T. Tran. 2025. "Evidence from East Asia on Pricing and Quantitative Low Carbon Policy Instruments." Unpublished paper.

Currie, J., and R. Walker. 2011. "Traffic Congestion and Infant Health: Evidence from E-ZPass. *American Economic Journal: Applied Economics* 3 (1): 65–90.

De Groote, O., A. Gautier, and F. Verboven. 2024. "The Political Economy of Financing Climate Policy: Evidence from the Solar PV Subsidy Programs." *Resource and Energy Economics* 77: 101436.

Dechezleprêtre, A., A. Fabre, T. Kruse, B. Planterose, A. S. Chico, and S. Stantcheva. Forthcoming. "Fighting Climate Change: International Attitudes toward Climate Policies." *American Economic Review.*

Gerarden, T. D. 2023. "Demanding Innovation: The Impact of Consumer Subsidies on Solar Panel Production Costs." *Management Science* 69 (12): 7799–820. https://doi.org/10.1287 /mnsc.2022.4662.

Graff Zivin, J., and M. Neidell. 2012. "The Impact of Pollution on Worker Productivity." *American Economic Review* 102 (7): 3652–73. https://doi.org/10.1257/aer.102.7.3652.

Hayashi, D., J. Huenteler, and J. I. Lewis. 2018. "Gone with the Wind: A Learning Curve Analysis of China's Wind Power Industry." *Energy Policy* 120: 38–51. https://doi .org/10.1016/j.enpol.2018.05.012.

Huenteler, J., T. Tang, G. Chan, and L. D. Anadon. 2018. "Why Is China's Wind Power Generation Not Living Up to Its Potential?" *Environmental Research Letters* 13 (4): 044001. https://doi.org/10.1088/1748-9326/aaadeb.

Johnstone, N., I. Haščič, and D. Popp. 2010. "Renewable Energy Policies and Technological Innovation: Evidence Based on Patent Counts." *Environmental and Resource Economics* 45: 133–55.

Larsen, K., H. Pitt, M. Mobir, S. Movalia, A. Rivera, E. Rutkowski, and T. Houser. 2023. "Global Emerging Climate Technology Diffusion and the Inflation Reduction Act." Rhodium Group, New York. https://rhg.com/research/emerging-climate-technology-ira/.

Martin, R., and D. Verhoeven. 2022. "Knowledge Spillovers from Clean and Emerging Technologies in the UK." *LSE Research Online Documents on Economics* 117804.

Neidell, M. J. 2004. "Air Pollution, Health, and Socio-Economic Status: The Effect of Outdoor Air Quality on Childhood Asthma." *Journal of Health Economics* 23 (6): 1209–36. https://doi.org/10.1016/j.jhealeco.2004.05.002.

Ren, S., H. Yang, Y. Hu, and J. Chevallier. 2022. "Emission Trading, Induced Innovation and Firm Performance." *Energy Economics* 112: 106157. https://doi.org/10.1016/j .eneco.2022.106157.

Rodrik, D. 2014. "Green Industrial Policy." *Oxford Review of Economic Policy* 30 (3): 469–91.

Rozenberg, J., A. Vogt-Schilb, and S. Hallegatte. 2020. "Instrument Choice and Stranded Assets in the Transition to Clean Capital." *Journal of Environmental Economics and Management* 100: 102183. https://doi.org/10.1016/j.jeem.2018.10.005.

Verhoeven, D., and R. Martin. 2024. "Knowledge Spillovers from Clean Innovation: A Tradeoff between Growth and Climate?" https://doi.org/10.21203/rs.3.rs-3663797/v1.

Carbon pricing schemes in East Asia and Pacific, by country

This appendix provides information on the carbon pricing schemes (emissions trading schemes and carbon taxes) in eight economies: China, Indonesia, Japan, the Republic of Korea, Malaysia, Singapore, Thailand, and Viet Nam. It is based on information from the World Bank Carbon Dashboard (https://carbonpricingdashboard.worldbank.org/).

China (emissions trading scheme)

Status and description

China implemented its emissions trading scheme (ETS) in 2021. It is the world's largest ETS in terms of covered emissions. The system builds on the subnational pilot carbon markets implemented in eight regions. Compliance obligations apply to entities in the power sector emitting over 26,000 tons of carbon dioxide (tCO_2) annually. The system covers more than 2,000 entities. The national market covers over 4,000 metric tons of carbon dioxide ($MtCO_2$). Entities regulated under the national system do not face compliance obligations under the pilot ETS. The "National Measures for the Administration of Carbon Emission Trading" describes the rules governing the ETS. Work on the national ETS trading platform and the CO_2 allowance registry is ongoing.

In January 2024, China launched its domestic offsetting scheme, the Chinese Certified Emissions Reduction (CCER) scheme, after six years of suspension, during which it underwent reform. In October 2023, the Ministry of Ecology and

Environment published the new regulations for the CCER. It also released four new methodologies, including on forestation, mangrove cultivation, solar thermal power, and grid-connected offshore wind power projects. In November 2023, the National Center for Climate Change Strategy Research and International Cooperation published guidelines for the CCER registry. The Beijing Green Exchange has also published guidelines for CCER trading and clearing. In February 2024, the State Council of the People's Republic of China published a regulation for the national ETS that significantly increased penalties for noncompliance, data fraud, and market manipulation behaviors.

In May 2021, the Ministry of Ecology and Environment announced the option of establishing a market-regulating and protection mechanism, which would allow it to respond to abnormal fluctuations in trading prices (through buy-backs, auctions, or adjustment of the rules related to use of the CCER program, for instance). The triggers and specifics of this mechanism have not yet been defined. Benchmarking is used as the main allocation method, with four distinct benchmarks: conventional coal plants below 300 megawatts (MW), conventional coal plants above 300 MW, unconventional coal, and natural gas. Entities received allowances at 70 percent of their 2021 verified emissions. Allocation was subsequently adjusted to reflect actual generation in 2021 and 2022. A unit load (output) adjustment factor distributed more allowances for entities operating at load rates lower than 85 percent. This change may have provided more allowances to less efficient power units. The cap is the sum of the bottom-up total allowance allocation to all individual covered entities. The cap changes according to the actual production levels.

Coverage

The ETS covers coal, diesel, gasoline, kerosene, other oil products, natural gas, liquefied petroleum gas (LPG), waste as fuel, and biofuels. It initially applies only to CO_2 emissions from the power sector, including combined heat and power and captive power plants from other sectors. It covers 32 percent of jurisdiction emissions (9.3 percent of global emissions).

Indonesia (emissions trading scheme)

Status and description

The Nilai Ekonomi Karbon (NEK) (Economic Value of Carbon) Trading Scheme is a mandatory, intensity-based, baseline-and-credit ETS for the power sector, launched in early 2023. In its first phase (2023–24), it targeted only coal-fired power plants connected to the Perusahaan Listrik Negara (PLN) grid with a capacity of 25 MW or more. In 2023, it covered 99 coal-fired power plants, estimated to represent around 81 percent of the country's power generation capacity. Covered entities are required to surrender allowances corresponding to all their covered emissions, with allocation based on intensity targets (Technical Emissions Ceiling Approvals, or Persetujuan Teknis Batas Atas Emisi [PTBAE]), emissions intensity, and average emissions. Entities have the option to purchase allowances via auctions.

Coverage

The ETS covers only coal. It covers 26 percent of jurisdiction emissions (0.6 percent of global emissions).

Japan (emissions trading scheme)

Japan began considering establishing an ETS in 2008; it has been developing the system since 2016. In March 2017, the Global Environment Committee of the Central Environment Council (an advisory committee to the Ministry of the Environment) formulated the "Long-Term Low-Carbon Vision" for the country. It refers to carbon pricing as essential to decarbonizing Japan. Based on that discussion, in March 2018 an expert committee on carbon pricing released a study assessing how carbon pricing could help Japan achieve substantial long-term emissions reductions as well as solve economic and social issues. In June 2018, a deliberative council (the Subcommittee on Utilization of Carbon Pricing, Global Environmental Subcommittee, Central Environment Council) was set up to consider how carbon pricing could spur Japan to make the transition to a decarbonized society and increase economic growth.

The Green Transformation (GX)-ETS started as a voluntary baseline-and-credit system in 2023. Almost 570 companies, collectively responsible for more than half of Japan's emissions, participate. Under the GX-ETS, J-Credits are traded on the Tokyo Stock Exchange.

The GX-ETS is expected to transition to a mandatory ETS in 2026, after its first compliance deadline. Japan plans to introduce upper and lower price limits. It plans to introduce auctioning for high-emitting entities in the power sector in 2033.

Japan (carbon tax)

Status and description

Japan began taxing carbon in 2012. The tax (officially known as the "tax for climate change mitigation") aims to impose an economywide and fair burden for the use of all fossil fuels based on their CO_2 content, in order to create a decarbonized society and strengthen climate change mitigation.

Coverage

The tax covers coal, diesel, gasoline, kerosene, other oil products, natural gas, and LPG. It applies to CO_2 emissions from the combustion of fossil fuels across all sectors, with some exemptions for the industry, power, agriculture, and transport sectors. The tax covers 80 percent of jurisdiction emissions (1.5 percent of global emissions).

Republic of Korea (emissions trading scheme)

Status and description

Korea implemented its ETS—the first national cap-and-trade system in East Asia—in 2015. It plays an essential role in ensuring that Korea meets its 2030 Nationally Determined Contribution (NDC) target. The Emissions Allowance Allocation Committee under the Ministry of Strategy and Finance determines the total amount of emission allowances.

In November 2022, the government announced several near-term changes to the ETS. They included increasing incentives to reduce emissions and facilitate low-carbon investment by issuing more free allowances to the most efficient covered entities; encouraging trading and mitigating price volatility by opening up the ETS to more financial firms and increasing the allowance holding limit; facilitating the conversion of international offset credits to Korean Credit Units; strengthening monitoring, reporting, and verification; and increasing support for small businesses and new entrants.

The Allocation Committee may implement market stabilization measures if certain conditions regarding a persistent supply–demand imbalance are met. They include auctioning allowances from the reserve, imposing banking limitations, changing the borrowing limits, changing the offset restrictions, and temporarily setting a price floor or ceiling. Auctions for market stability will be subject to an auction reserve price. In 2023, the government set two temporary price floors. The trigger price remained at an average of ₩12,088 (US$9.26), calculated as 60 percent of the average price in the preceding two years. The first price floor, of ₩7,020 (US$5.38), was established in July 2023; the last, of ₩7,750 (US$5.94), was set in November 2023 and lifted in early December 2023, when prices were maintained at ₩8,520 (US$6.53) for five consecutive days.

As of the start of 2024, there were eight K-ETS market makers. These institutions can draw on a government-held reserve of 20 million allowances to increase liquidity in the market. A cap limits the total emissions allowed in the system. Caps for 2023, 2024, and 2025 are 589.3, 567.1, and 567.1 $MtCO_2e$, respectively. Regular auctions began in 2019; free allocation is used alongside auctioning.

Coverage

The ETS covers coal, diesel, gasoline, kerosene, other oil products, natural gas, LPG, biofuels, and emissions not from fuel use. It applies to emissions of CO_2, methane, nitrous oxide, perfluorochemicals, hydrofluorocarbons, and sulfur hexafluorides from the industry, power, buildings, domestic aviation, public, and waste sectors. Emissions- and/or trade-intensive sectors at risk of carbon leakage receive free allowances of up to 100 percent of the benchmark or historical emission level. Some small emitters are exempt from the ETS, which covers 89 percent of jurisdiction emissions (1.2 percent of global emissions).

Malaysia (emissions trading scheme and carbon tax)

The government began preliminary work in 2023 to investigate the potential for a carbon tax and an ETS. It plans to launch voluntary offset trading before rolling out a domestic ETS. It has released "National Guidance on International Voluntary Carbon Market Mechanisms" to Malaysian entities planning to engage in carbon market activities.

The Malaysian Stock Exchange launched the Bursa Carbon Exchange, the world's first *shariah*-compliant voluntary carbon market platform, in December 2022. The Bursa Carbon Exchange completed the country's first carbon credit auction on March 16, 2023.

Singapore (carbon tax)

Status and description

Singapore implemented its carbon tax in 2019. It applies to all facilities with annual direct greenhouse gas emissions of 25 $ktCO_2e$ or more, with no exemptions. Revenue from the tax supports initiatives to address climate change. Since January 1, 2024, companies have been able to surrender high-quality international carbon credits to offset up to 5 percent of their taxable emissions.

Coverage

The tax covers coal, diesel, gasoline, kerosene, other oil products, natural gas, LPG, jet fuel, waste as fuel, biofuels, and emissions not from fuel use. It applies to direct emissions of CO_2, methane, nitrous oxide, sulphur hexafluoride, hydrofluorocarbons, and perfluorocarbons by all facilities emitting 25 $ktCO_2e$ or more in a year. In addition, excise duties are levied on transport fuels; they serve as a carbon price signal for transportation emissions.

Singapore intends to introduce a transition framework to provide existing facilities in emissions-intensive trade-exposed sectors with transitory allowances for part of their emissions, based on efficiency standards and decarbonization targets. Companies can also continue to tap existing support measures for decarbonization, such as the Resource Efficiency Grant for Energy, Investment Allowances for Emissions Reduction, and the Energy Efficiency Fund.

On January 1, 2024, Singapore introduced three changes. First, it increased the carbon tax rate to S$25/$tCO_2e$ for 2024 and 2025 and S$45/$tCO_2e$ for 2026 and 2027, with a view to reaching S$50–S$80/tCO_2e by 2030. Second, it extended the carbon tax coverage to include nitrogen trifluoride emissions. Third, it introduced a transition framework, to give existing emissions-intensive trade-exposed companies more time to adjust to a low-carbon economy. These firms receive transitory allowances for part of their emissions, based on efficiency standards and decarbonization targets.

Thailand (emissions trading scheme)

The government has been assessing various types of carbon pricing initiatives since 2016. As part of this process, it established a voluntary ETS, which aims to develop and test monitoring, reporting, and verification systems; cap-setting and allocation procedures; and trading infrastructure for 12 greenhouse gas–intensive sectors. Targets are set for each sector based on average emissions intensity in the base years of 2012–13. The system covers both direct and indirect emissions.

In 2021, the voluntary ETS pilot project was extended to the Eastern Economic Corridor area, a key industrial region of Thailand. ETS capacity-building programs were implemented in several pilot organizations.

Viet Nam (emissions trading scheme)

Viet Nam has been considering designing a domestic ETS and a national crediting mechanism since 2017. In July 2022, it issued a decision that committed it to achieving net-zero emissions by 2050, with a midterm target of 43.5 percent below the baseline by 2030. This decision followed Decree 06/2022/ND-CP, which outlined a road map for implementing an ETS with a declining cap corresponding to Viet Nam's NDC. On January 24, 2025, Viet Nam approved the road map for ETS implementation. A pilot ETS is scheduled to start in June 2025, with full implementation set for 2029.

www.ingramcontent.com/pod-product-compliance
Lightning Source LLC
Chambersburg PA
CBHW042058210326
41597CB00045B/60